The New Grammar in Action
Assessment

Caroline T. Linse
Barbara Edwards

HEINLE & HEINLE

★
™

THOMSON LEARNING

United States • Australia • Canada • Mexico • Singapore • Spain • United Kingdom

HEINLE & HEINLE

THOMSON LEARNING

The New Grammar in Action
Assessment

Vice President, Editorial Director ESL/EFL: Nancy Leonhardt

Marketing Manager: Eric Bredenberg

Senior Production Editor: Maryellen E. Killeen

Developmental Editor: Thomas Healy

Senior Manufacturing Coordinator: Mary Beth Hennebury

Design/Production: Laurel Tech

Acquisitions Editor: Sherrise Roehr

Cover Design: Rotunda Design/Gina Petti

Illustration: Dave Blanchette

Printer: The Mazer Corporation

Copyright © 2001 Heinle & Heinle, a division of Thomson Learning, Inc.
Thomson Learning™ is a trademark used herein under license.

Printed in the United States of America
1 2 3 4 5 6 7 8 9 10 05 04 03 02 01

For more information, contact Heinle & Heinle Publishers, 20 Park Plaza, Boston, MA 02116 USA,
or you can visit our Internet site at http://www.heinle.com

For permission to use material from this text or product, contact us:
Tel   (800) 730-2214
Fax   (800) 730-2215
Web www.thomsonrights.com

ISBN: 0-8384-1123-1

Table of Contents

Basic

Basic—Unit 1

Name _____ **Date** _____

Select the word or words that match each picture.

Example: 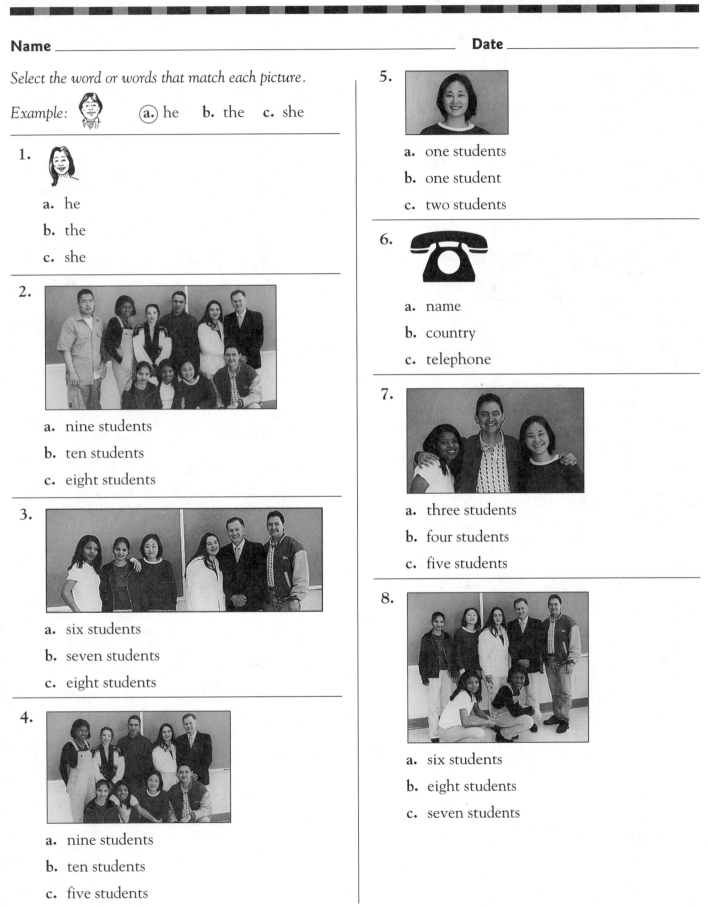 **a.** he **b.** the **c.** she

1.
- **a.** he
- **b.** the
- **c.** she

2.
- **a.** nine students
- **b.** ten students
- **c.** eight students

3.
- **a.** six students
- **b.** seven students
- **c.** eight students

4.
- **a.** nine students
- **b.** ten students
- **c.** five students

5.
- **a.** one students
- **b.** one student
- **c.** two students

6.
- **a.** name
- **b.** country
- **c.** telephone

7.
- **a.** three students
- **b.** four students
- **c.** five students

8.
- **a.** six students
- **b.** eight students
- **c.** seven students

9.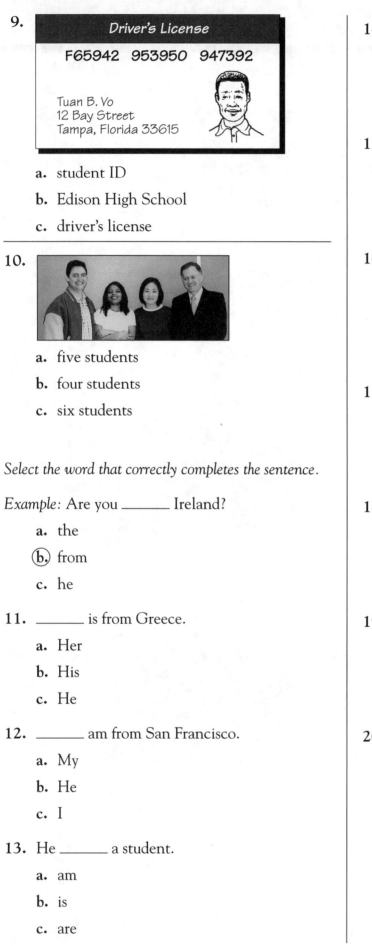

Driver's License

F65942 953950 947392

Tuan B. Vo
12 Bay Street
Tampa, Florida 33615

   a. student ID

   b. Edison High School

   c. driver's license

10.

   a. five students

   b. four students

   c. six students

Select the word that correctly completes the sentence.

Example: Are you _____ Ireland?

   a. the

   ⓑ. from

   c. he

11. _____ is from Greece.

   a. Her

   b. His

   c. He

12. _____ am from San Francisco.

   a. My

   b. He

   c. I

13. He _____ a student.

   a. am

   b. is

   c. are

14. I _____ a student.

   a. am

   b. is

   c. are

15. She _____ a student.

   a. am

   b. is

   c. are

16. Her first name is Mary, her last _____ is Smith.

   a. country

   b. Student

   c. name

17. His student ID number is _____.

   a. 4372154

   b. Cortes

   c. Winston

18. Where are you _____?

   a. name

   b. student

   c. from

19. _____ your name?

   a. Where

   b. Is

   c. What's

20. _____ is from Ireland.

   a. She

   b. Her

   c. If

Basic—Unit 2

Name _____ Date _____

Select the word or words that match each picture.

Example: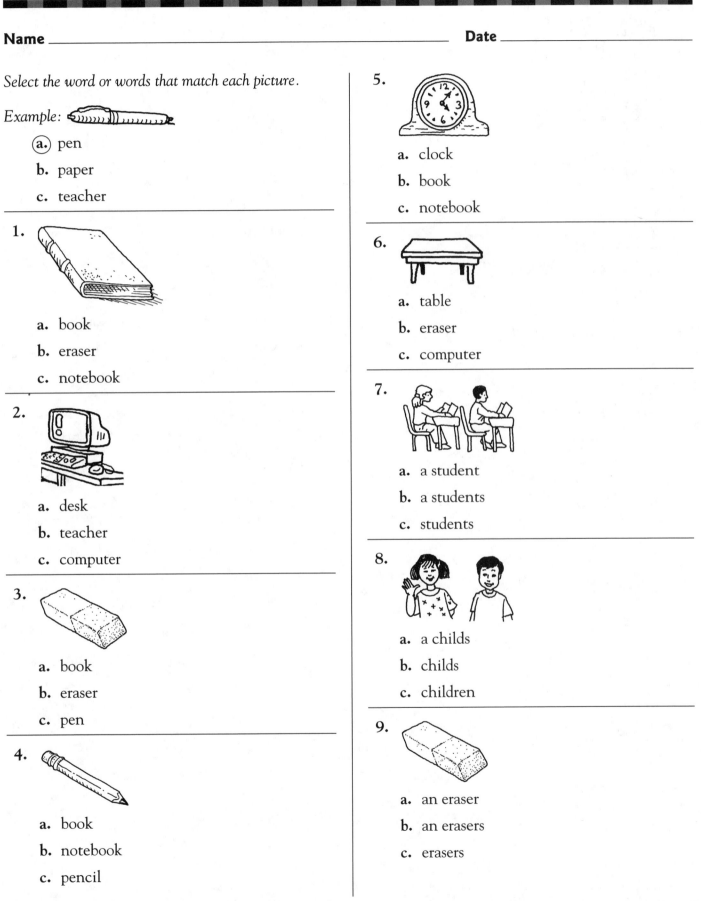

   (a.) pen

   b. paper

   c. teacher

1.

   a. book

   b. eraser

   c. notebook

2.

   a. desk

   b. teacher

   c. computer

3.

   a. book

   b. eraser

   c. pen

4.

   a. book

   b. notebook

   c. pencil

5.

   a. clock

   b. book

   c. notebook

6.

   a. table

   b. eraser

   c. computer

7.

   a. a student

   b. a students

   c. students

8.

   a. a childs

   b. childs

   c. children

9.

   a. an eraser

   b. an erasers

   c. erasers

10.

    a. a man

    b. a men

    c. mans

Select the word or words that best complete the sentence.

Example: This is a _____ sharpener.

    (**a.**) pencil

    b. eraser

    c. erasers

11. _____ this your book?

    a. Are

    b. Am

    c. Is

12. Yes, it _____.

    a. are

    b. is

    c. am

13. No, it _____.

    a. aren't

    b. isn't

    c. not

14. There are _____ erasers.

    a. three

    b. one

    c. a

15. _____ twenty students.

    a. Are

    b. There is

    c. There are

16. There are fifteen _____ in the room.

    a. room

    b. maps

    c. map

17. There are six _____ in the class.

    a. children

    b. child

    c. childs

18. There _____ a book on the desk.

    a. is

    b. are

    c. it

19. There _____ nineteen students in the room.

    a. is

    b. are

    c. it

20. There is one student from _____.

    a. eraser

    b. China

    c. pencil

Name _____ **Date** _____

Select the word or words that match each picture.

Example:

(a.) grandfather

b. grandmother

c. sister

1.

a. father

b. brother

c. mother

2.

a. wife

b. husband

c. grandmother

3.

a. brother

b. sister

c. daughter

4.

a. grandfather

b. grandmother

c. husband

5.

a. daughter

b. son

c. father

6.

January **February** **March**

a. days

b. hours

c. months

Select the word or words that correctly complete the sentence.

Example: How old are _____?

a. she

b. he

(c.) you

7. _____ seven.

a. He

b. He's

c. Him

8. I _____ in Miami.

a. living

b. lives

c. live

9. They _____ in Japan.

    a. living

    b. lives

    c. live

10. She _____ in Chicago.

    a. lives

    b. living

    c. live

11. How old _____ he?

    a. am

    b. are

    c. is

12. _____ twenty.

    a. She

    b. She's

    c. Her

13. Where _____ you live?

    a. does

    b. doing

    c. do

14. Where _____ they live?

    a. does

    b. doing

    c. do

15. Where _____ he live?

    a. does

    b. doing

    c. do

16. Where _____ she live?

    a. does

    b. doing

    c. do

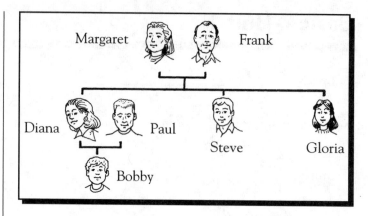

Look at the picture. For numbers 17, 18, 19, and 20, select the word or words that correctly complete the sentence.

17. Margaret and Frank are _____.

    a. sisters

    b. brothers

    c. parents

18. Paul and Steve are _____.

    a. brothers

    b. sisters

    c. daughters

19. Diana and Gloria are _____.

    a. sisters-in-law

    b. brothers

    c. divorced

20. Margaret and Gloria are _____.

    a. mother and daughter

    b. brothers

    c. grandfathers

Basic—Unit 4

Name _____ **Date** _____

Select the word or words that match each picture.

Example:

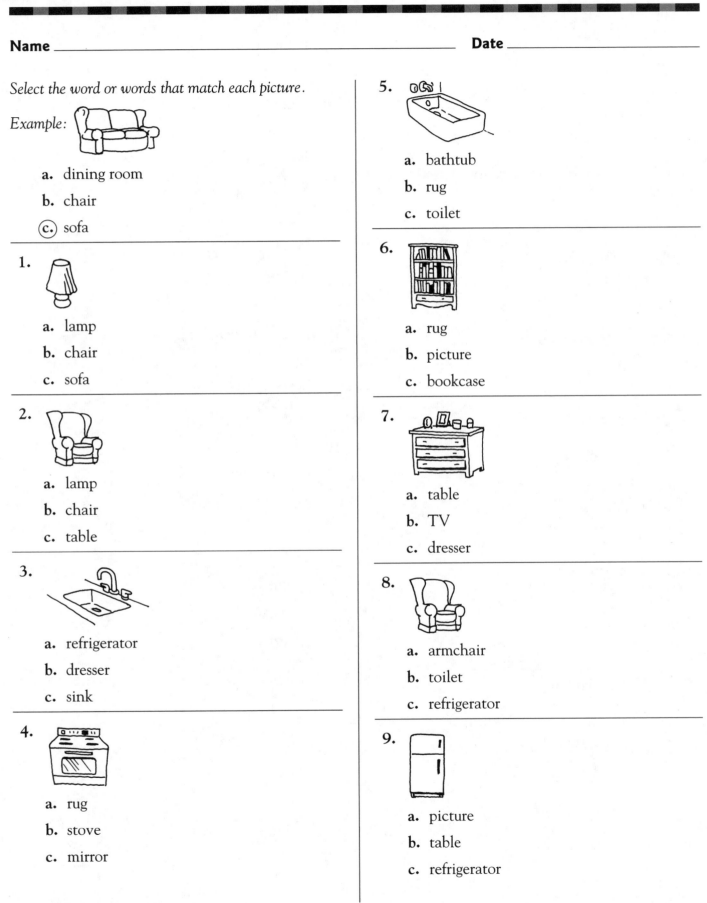

a. dining room

b. chair

(c.) sofa

1.

a. lamp

b. chair

c. sofa

2.

a. lamp

b. chair

c. table

3.

a. refrigerator

b. dresser

c. sink

4.

a. rug

b. stove

c. mirror

5.

a. bathtub

b. rug

c. toilet

6.

a. rug

b. picture

c. bookcase

7.

a. table

b. TV

c. dresser

8.

a. armchair

b. toilet

c. refrigerator

9.

a. picture

b. table

c. refrigerator

10.

    a. TV

    b. bed

    c. shower

Select the word or words that correctly completes the sentence.

Example: I have a _____.

    (**a.**) dresser

    b. needing

    c. eat

11. I _____ a sofa.

    a. needs

    b. needing

    c. need

12. I _____ a microwave.

    a. don't

    b. don't have

    c. do

13. I _____ studying.

    a. am

    b. are

    c. is

14. He _____ working.

    a. am

    b. are

    c. is

15. They _____ eating.

    a. am

    b. are

    c. is

16. Yes, I _____.

    a. am

    b. are

    c. is

17. No, _____ not.

    a. I's

    b. I'm

    c. I'r

18. _____ he watching TV?

    a. Are

    b. Am

    c. Is

19. _____ you eating hamburgers?

    a. Are

    b. Am

    c. Is

20. _____ is she doing?

    a. What

    b. Where

    c. What's

Basic—Unit 5

Select the word or words that match each picture.

Example:

a. bank
b. bakery
c. drugstore

1.

a. library
b. police station
c. park

2.

a. shoe store
b. bakery
c. coffee shop

3.

a. shoes
b. drug store
c. library

4.

a. coffee shop
b. library
c. City Hall

5.

a. shoe store
b. parking lot
c. post office

6.

a. drugstore
b. bookstore
c. bell

7.

a. bookstore
b. shoe store
c. Laundromat

8.

   a. shoe store

   b. police station

   c. hospital

9.

   a. shoe store

   b. City Hall

   c. Laundromat

10.

   a. supermarket

   b. City Hall

   c. Laundromat

Select the best word or words to complete the sentence.

Example: The children are standing _____ the library.

   a. from across

   b. in front

   ⓒ across from

11. Mrs Gomez is _____ the store.

   a. at behind

   b. of behind

   c. behind

12. Laura is standing _____ the coffee shop.

   a. from across

   b. of across

   c. across from

13. The bus is parked _____ of the school.

   a. in front

   b. between

   c. of across

14. The children need to stand _____ their teacher.

   a. between

   b. behind

   c. of across

15. _____ were you with?

   a. What's

   b. Where

   c. Who

16. _____ are the children?

   a. What's

   b. Where

   c. When

17. _____ is eating donuts?

   a. Who

   b. Where

   c. What's

18. _____ buy books?

   a. Where can

   b. Who can I

   c. Where can I

19. It is _____ from 9 to 5.

   a. opening

   b. open

   c. closing

20. You _____ a park at 7th and Oak Streets.

   a. can find

   b. finding

   c. finds

Name _____ **Date** _____

Select the word or words that match each picture.

Example:

a. cashier

b. florist

(c.) manicurist

1.

a. cook

b. cashier

c. florist

2.

a. cook

b. security guard

c. salesperson

3.

a. waiter

b. cashier

c. painter

4.

a. cook

b. painter

c. pharmacist

5.

a. painter

b. cashier

c. salesperson

6.

a. pharmacist

b. painter

c. photographer

7.

a. beautician

b. cook

c. pharmacist

8.

  a. pharmacist

  b. cashier

  c. custodian

9.

  a. photographer

  b. cook

  c. salesperson

10.

  a. waiter

  b. photographer

  c. writer

Select the best word to complete the sentence.

Example: A custodian _____ the floor.

  a. cuts

  b. watches

  ⓒ sweeps

11. A florist _____ flowers.

  a. watches

  b. sells

  c. colors

12. A cook _____ food.

  a. prepares

  b. sweeps

  c. watches

13. A pharmacist _____ prescriptions.

  a. fills

  b. colors

  c. watches

14. A manicurist _____ nails.

  a. fills

  b. takes

  c. colors

15. A photographer _____ pictures.

  a. takes

  b. fills

  c. sweeps

16. Today, I _____ a teacher.

  a. am

  b. are

  c. is

17. I _____ up at 6:00 every day.

  a. gets

  b. getting

  c. get

18. They get up _____ 9:45.

  a. at

  b. is

  c. from

19. What _____ she do?

  a. does

  b. do

  c. doing

20. Where _____ he work?

  a. do

  b. does

  c. doing

14

Basic—Unit 7

Select the word or words that match each picture.

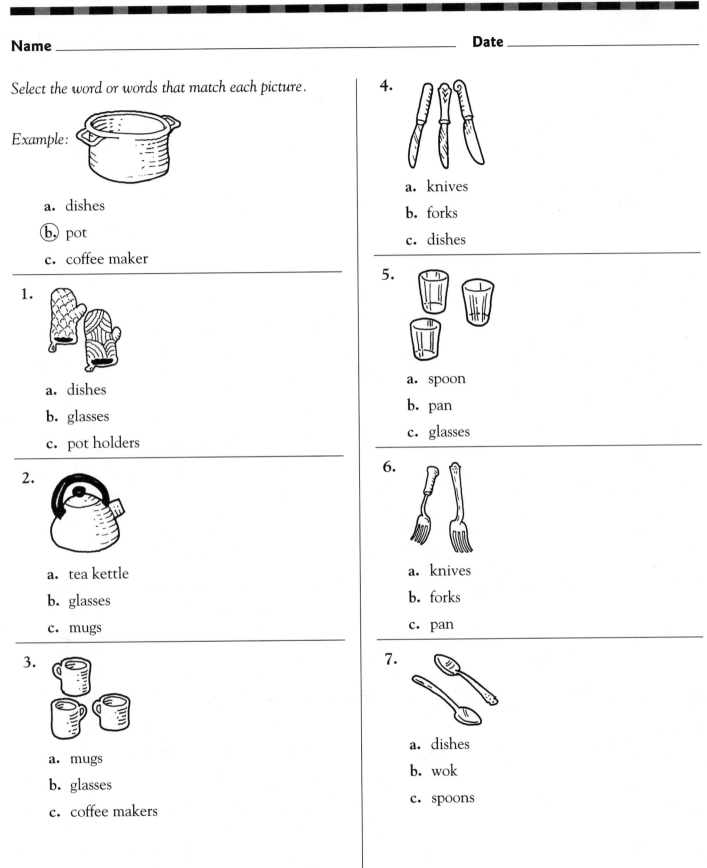

Example:

a. dishes

b. pot

c. coffee maker

1.

a. dishes

b. glasses

c. pot holders

2.

a. tea kettle

b. glasses

c. mugs

3.

a. mugs

b. glasses

c. coffee makers

4.

a. knives

b. forks

c. dishes

5.

a. spoon

b. pan

c. glasses

6.

a. knives

b. forks

c. pan

7.

a. dishes

b. wok

c. spoons

8.

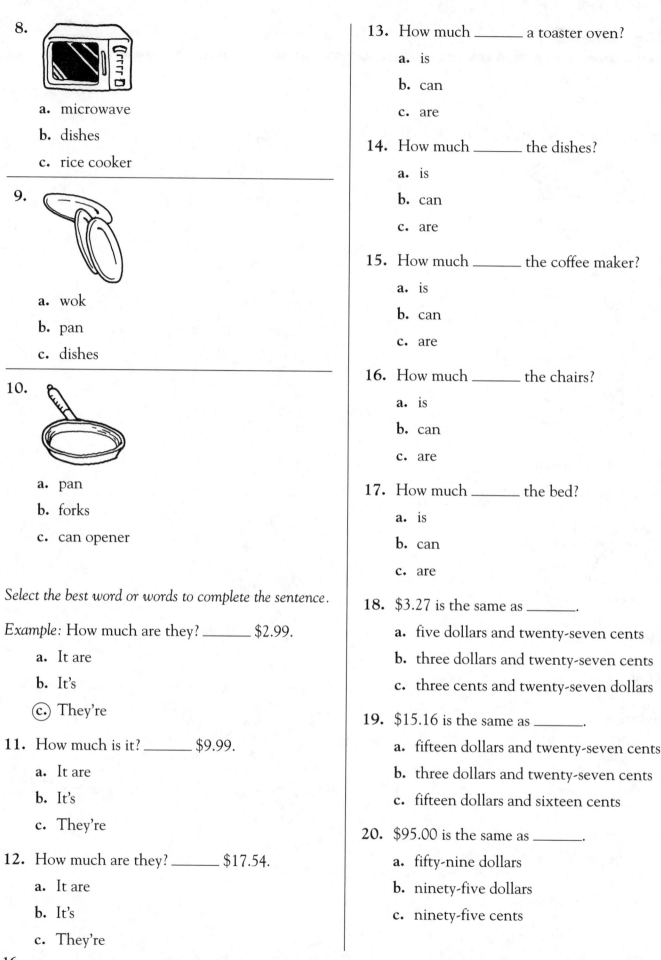

    a. microwave

    b. dishes

    c. rice cooker

9.

    a. wok

    b. pan

    c. dishes

10.

    a. pan

    b. forks

    c. can opener

Select the best word or words to complete the sentence.

Example: How much are they? _____ $2.99.

    a. It are

    b. It's

    c. They're

11. How much is it? _____ $9.99.

    a. It are

    b. It's

    c. They're

12. How much are they? _____ $17.54.

    a. It are

    b. It's

    c. They're

13. How much _____ a toaster oven?

    a. is

    b. can

    c. are

14. How much _____ the dishes?

    a. is

    b. can

    c. are

15. How much _____ the coffee maker?

    a. is

    b. can

    c. are

16. How much _____ the chairs?

    a. is

    b. can

    c. are

17. How much _____ the bed?

    a. is

    b. can

    c. are

18. $3.27 is the same as _____.

    a. five dollars and twenty-seven cents

    b. three dollars and twenty-seven cents

    c. three cents and twenty-seven dollars

19. $15.16 is the same as _____.

    a. fifteen dollars and twenty-seven cents

    b. three dollars and twenty-seven cents

    c. fifteen dollars and sixteen cents

20. $95.00 is the same as _____.

    a. fifty-nine dollars

    b. ninety-five dollars

    c. ninety-five cents

Name _____ **Date** _____

Select the word that matches each picture.

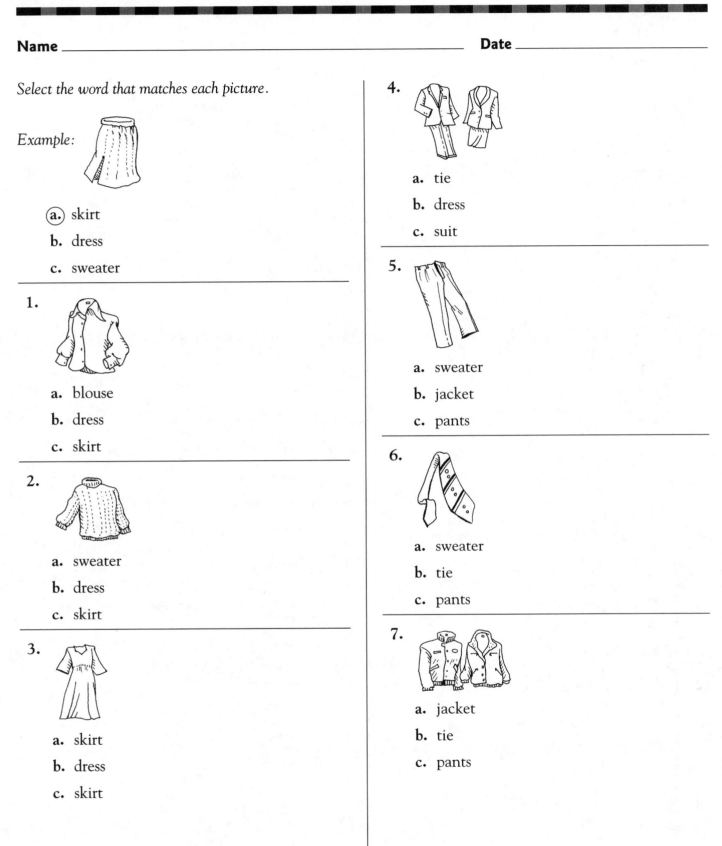

Example:

Ⓐ skirt

b. dress

c. sweater

1.

a. blouse

b. dress

c. skirt

2.

a. sweater

b. dress

c. skirt

3.

a. skirt

b. dress

c. skirt

4.

a. tie

b. dress

c. suit

5.

a. sweater

b. jacket

c. pants

6.

a. sweater

b. tie

c. pants

7.

a. jacket

b. tie

c. pants

8.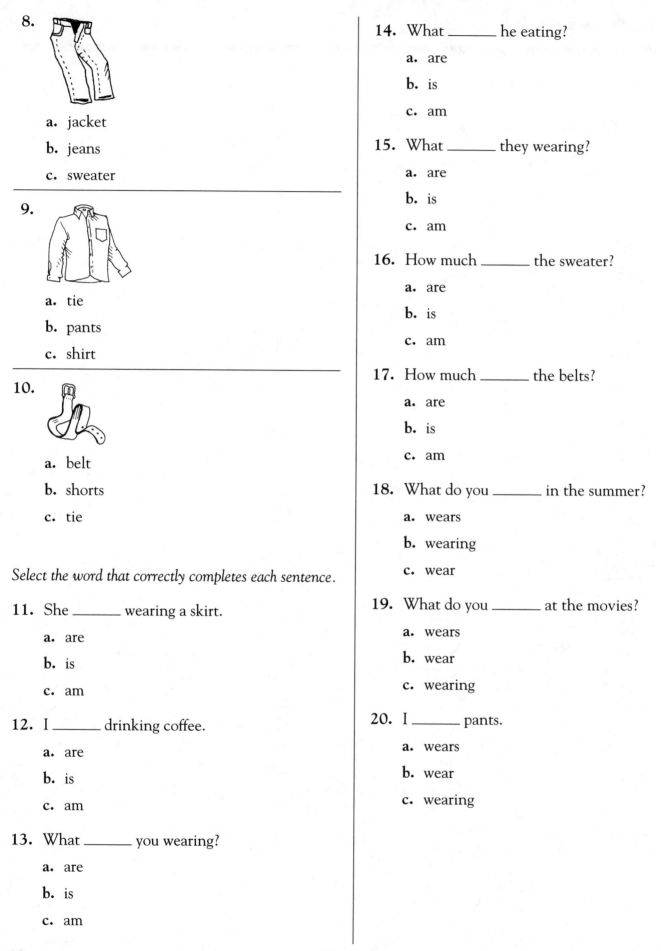

    a. jacket

    b. jeans

    c. sweater

9.

    a. tie

    b. pants

    c. shirt

10.

    a. belt

    b. shorts

    c. tie

Select the word that correctly completes each sentence.

11. She _____ wearing a skirt.

    a. are

    b. is

    c. am

12. I _____ drinking coffee.

    a. are

    b. is

    c. am

13. What _____ you wearing?

    a. are

    b. is

    c. am

14. What _____ he eating?

    a. are

    b. is

    c. am

15. What _____ they wearing?

    a. are

    b. is

    c. am

16. How much _____ the sweater?

    a. are

    b. is

    c. am

17. How much _____ the belts?

    a. are

    b. is

    c. am

18. What do you _____ in the summer?

    a. wears

    b. wearing

    c. wear

19. What do you _____ at the movies?

    a. wears

    b. wear

    c. wearing

20. I _____ pants.

    a. wears

    b. wear

    c. wearing

Basic—Unit 9

Name _____ Date _____

Select the word or words that match each picture.

Example:

(a.) donut
b. salad
c. cereal

1.

a. donut
b. eggs
c. pancakes

2.

a. hamburger
b. soup
c. bacon

3.

a. cereal
b. toast
c. soup

4.

a. pancakes
b. donut
c. cereal

5.

a. soup
b. salad
c. ham

6.

a. French fries
b. hamburger
c. salad

7.

a. soup
b. hamburger
c. salad

8.

a. toast
b. ham
c. donut

9.

a. hamburger
b. cereal
c. French fries

10.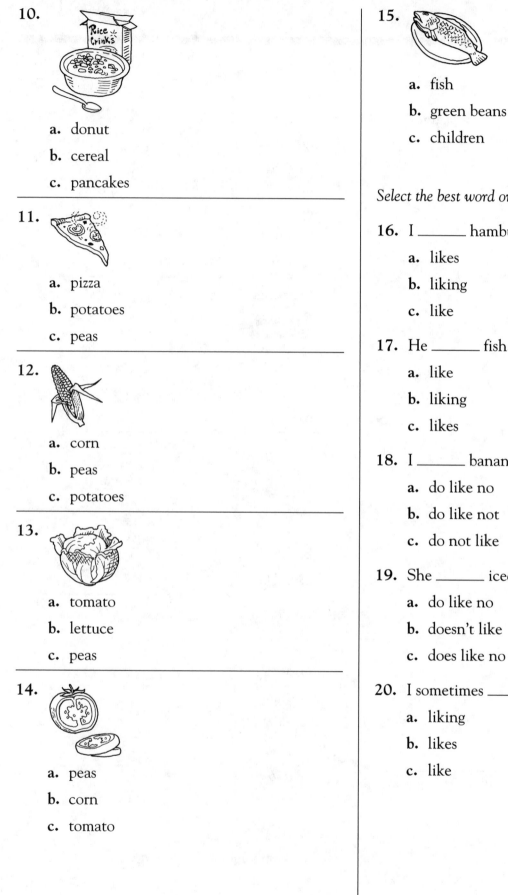

  a. donut

  b. cereal

  c. pancakes

11.

  a. pizza

  b. potatoes

  c. peas

12.

  a. corn

  b. peas

  c. potatoes

13.

  a. tomato

  b. lettuce

  c. peas

14.

  a. peas

  b. corn

  c. tomato

15.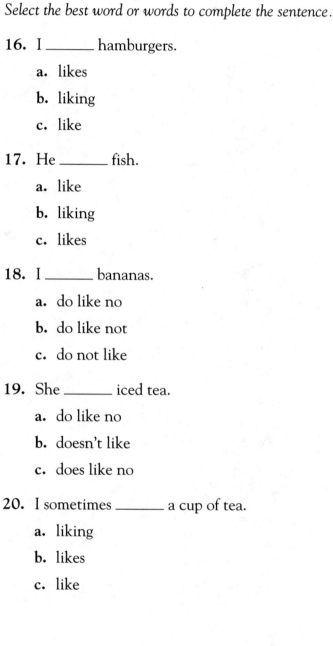

  a. fish

  b. green beans

  c. children

Select the best word or words to complete the sentence.

16. I _____ hamburgers.

  a. likes

  b. liking

  c. like

17. He _____ fish.

  a. like

  b. liking

  c. likes

18. I _____ bananas.

  a. do like no

  b. do like not

  c. do not like

19. She _____ iced tea.

  a. do like no

  b. doesn't like

  c. does like no

20. I sometimes _____ a cup of tea.

  a. liking

  b. likes

  c. like

Basic—Unit 10

Select the word or words that match each picture.

Example:

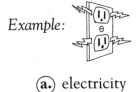

   a. electricity

   b. sunny

   c. from

1.

   a. dark

   b. sunny

   c. dirty

2.

   a. electricity

   b. lights

   c. faucet

3.

   a. The paint is peeling.

   b. The faucet is leaking.

   c. There are cockroaches.

4.

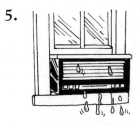

   a. noisy

   b. oven

   c. quiet

5.

   a. The lock is broken.

   b. The lights are broken.

   c. The air conditioner isn't working.

6.

   a. faucet

   b. lights

   c. window

7.

   a. The faucet is leaking.

   b. The paint is peeling.

   c. The heat is off.

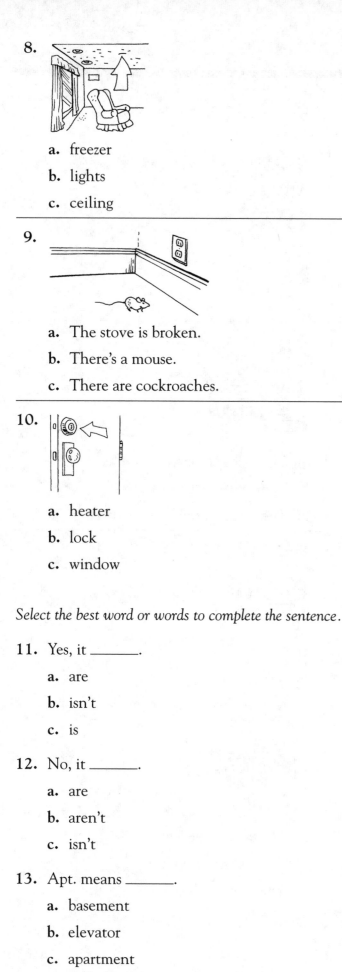

8.

a. freezer

b. lights

c. ceiling

9.

a. The stove is broken.

b. There's a mouse.

c. There are cockroaches.

10.

a. heater

b. lock

c. window

Select the best word or words to complete the sentence.

11. Yes, it _____.

a. are

b. isn't

c. is

12. No, it _____.

a. are

b. aren't

c. isn't

13. Apt. means _____.

a. basement

b. elevator

c. apartment

14. W/D means _____.

a. washer/dryer

b. air conditioning

c. basement

15. A/C means _____.

a. washer/dryer

b. air conditioning

c. basement

> Lge. 2BR, w/new W/D, sunny, pets OK, include utils., sec. dep., elev., new carpet, $750/mo.

Read the ad and then select the word or words that correctly complete each sentence.

16. It is _____.

a. small

b. medium

c. large

17. There is an _____.

a. washers and dryers

b. elevator

c. transportation

18. The rent is _____.

a. $650

b. $750

c. $1000

19. It has _____.

a. three bedrooms

b. two bedrooms

c. one bedroom

20. There is a _____.

a. washer/dryer

b. elevators

c. bedrooms

Name _____ **Date** _____

Select the word or words that match each picture.

Example:

   a. singer

   b. cook

   c. desk clerk

1.

   a. singer

   b. cook

   c. valet

2.

   a. desk clerk

   b. valet

   c. waiter

3.

   a. piano player

   b. waiter

   c. valet

4.

   a. desk clerk

   b. landscaper

   c. waiter

5.

   a. housekeeper

   b. waiter

   c. singer

6.

   a. landscaper

   b. singer

   c. coat

7.

   a. waitress

   b. bartender

   c. bellhop

8.

a. desk clerk

b. bartender

c. laundry worker

9.

a. bartender

b. landscaper

c. laundry worker

10.

a. waiter

b. waitress

c. bellhop

Select the best word or words to complete the sentence.

11. A _____ washes sheets and towels.

  a. laundry worker

  b. bellhop

  c. waitress

12. A _____ registers guests.

  a. desk clerk

  b. waitress

  c. waiter

13. A _____ takes food orders.

  a. waiter

  b. laundry worker

  c. valet

14. A _____ carries bags.

  a. waiter

  b. waitress

  c. bellhop

15. A _____ sings songs.

  a. housekeeper

  b. singer

  c. laundry worker

16. Yes, he _____.

  a. do

  b. doesn't

  c. does

17. No, he _____.

  a. doesn't

  b. do

  c. does

18. I _____ medical benefits.

  a. has

  b. no have

  c. don't have

19. I _____ dental benefits.

  a. also

  b. has no

  c. don't have

20. I _____ a bellhop from 1990–2000.

  a. work

  b. was

  c. has

Basic—Unit 12

Select the word or words that match each picture.

Example:

   a. hot

   b. windy

   c. cool

1.

   a. I walk.

   b. I ride my bike.

   c. I take the train.

2.

   a. I take the subway.

   b. I walk.

   c. I take a taxi.

3.

   a. I drive.

   b. I take the bus.

   c. I take the train.

4.

   a. I drive.

   b. I walk.

   c. I take the subway.

5.

   a. It's sunny.

   b. It's raining.

   c. It's snowing.

6.

   a. It's hot.

   b. It's cool.

   c. It's cold.

7.

   a. It's sunny.

   b. It's raining.

   c. It's cloudy.

8.

   a. It's hot.

   b. It's sunny.

   c. It's cold.

9.

   a. It's windy.

   b. It's cloudy.

   c. It's raining.

10.

   a. It's snowing.

   b. It's cloudy.

   c. It's raining.

Select the best word or words to complete the sentence.

Example: Drive _____.

   ⓐ three blocks

   b. turn

   c. walk

11. Turn _____.

   a. block

   b. left

   c. park

12. I _____ going to work.

   a. am

   b. is

   c. are

13. You _____ going to bed.

   a. am

   b. is

   c. are

14. They _____ going to the park.

   a. am

   b. is

   c. are

15. He _____ going home.

   a. am

   b. is

   c. are

16. _____ do you get to work?

   a. Who

   b. What

   c. How

17. You _____ park here.

   a. must

   b. must is

   c. must no

18. You _____ stop.

   a. no must

   b. must no

   c. must not

19. _____ warm and sunny.

   a. It

   b. It's

   c. It are

20. Where _____ Anita going?

   a. am

   b. is

   c. are

Basic—Unit 13

Select the word or words that match each picture.

Example:

- **(a.)** teeth
- **b.** feet
- **c.** thumb

1.

- **a.** leg
- **b.** toes
- **c.** eyes

2.

- **a.** thumb
- **b.** teeth
- **c.** hip

3.

- **a.** lips
- **b.** hip
- **c.** back

4.

- **a.** toes
- **b.** chin
- **c.** fingers

5.

- **a.** dentist
- **b.** ice pack
- **c.** healing

6.

- **a.** ibuprofen
- **b.** sore throat
- **c.** ice pack

7.

- **a.** stomachache
- **b.** headache
- **c.** aspirin

8.

- **a.** aspirin
- **b.** ibuprofen
- **c.** cough

9.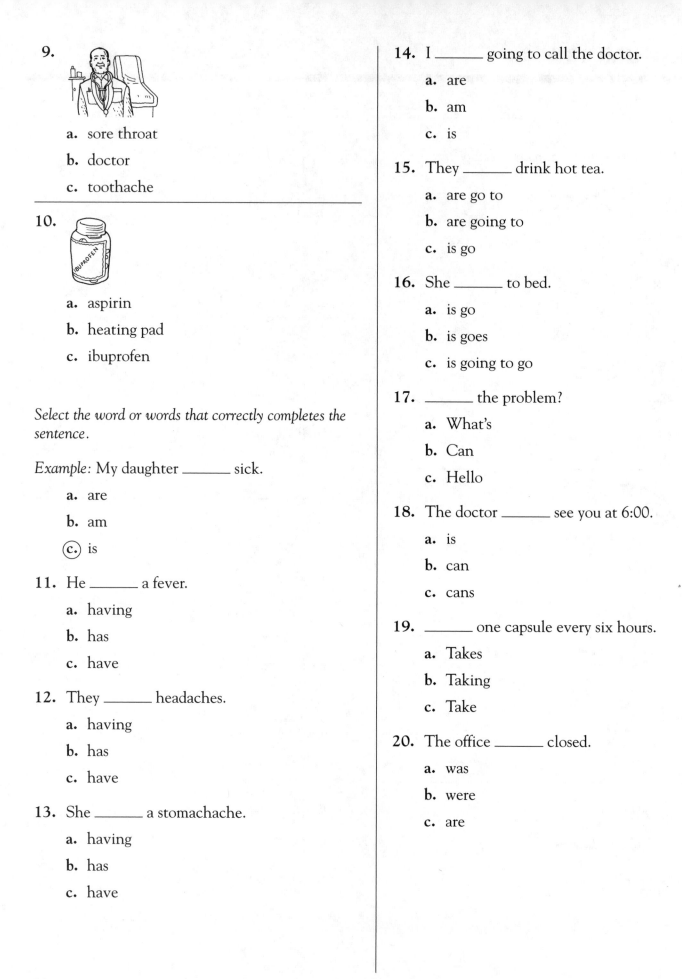

    a. sore throat

    b. doctor

    c. toothache

10.

    a. aspirin

    b. heating pad

    c. ibuprofen

Select the word or words that correctly completes the sentence.

Example: My daughter _____ sick.

    a. are

    b. am

    ⓒ is

11. He _____ a fever.

    a. having

    b. has

    c. have

12. They _____ headaches.

    a. having

    b. has

    c. have

13. She _____ a stomachache.

    a. having

    b. has

    c. have

14. I _____ going to call the doctor.

    a. are

    b. am

    c. is

15. They _____ drink hot tea.

    a. are go to

    b. are going to

    c. is go

16. She _____ to bed.

    a. is go

    b. is goes

    c. is going to go

17. _____ the problem?

    a. What's

    b. Can

    c. Hello

18. The doctor _____ see you at 6:00.

    a. is

    b. can

    c. cans

19. _____ one capsule every six hours.

    a. Takes

    b. Taking

    c. Take

20. The office _____ closed.

    a. was

    b. were

    c. are

Basic—Unit 14

Select the word or words that match each picture.

Example:

a. desk clerk
b. gardener
c. custodian

1.

a. bellhop
b. gardener
c. nurse's aide

2.

a. waiter
b. electrician
c. nurse's aide

3.

a. nurse's aide
b. laundry worker
c. gardener

4.

a. ear
b. earplug
c. plug

5.

a. screwdriver
b. hammer
c. flashlight

6.

a. mop
b. mixer
c. broom

7.

a. microwave
b. oven
c. nametag

8.

a. cable
b. shirt
c. gloves

9.

    a. mixer

    b. cook

    c. waiter

10.

    a. head

    b. mask

    c. hard hat

Select the best word or words to complete each sentence.

Example: Melissa _____ a cold.

    (a.) caught

    b. broke down

    c. threw

11. My car _____.

    a. cancelled

    b. broke down

    c. missed

12. Joseph _____ the bus.

    a. down

    b. missed

    c. overslept

13. I _____ gloves.

    a. was

    b. wore

    c. weren't

14. They _____ watching TV.

    a. was

    b. wasn't

    c. weren't

15. She _____ wearing gloves.

    a. was

    b. weren't

    c. hasn't

16. I _____ wear a mask.

    a. has to

    b. don't has to

    c. don't have to

17. They _____ wear hard hats.

    a. have to

    b. has to

    c. don't has to

18. You _____ wear a name tag.

    a. don't has to

    b. have to

    c. has to

19. Phil _____ confirm his assistance.

    a. have to

    b. doesn't have to

    c. doesn't has to

20. I _____ aware of that requirement.

    a. were

    b. can

    c. wasn't

Basic—Unit 15

Select the word or words that match each picture.

Example: 15+12=
20-4=
2x+4x=

a. math *(circled)*
b. color
c. play an instrument

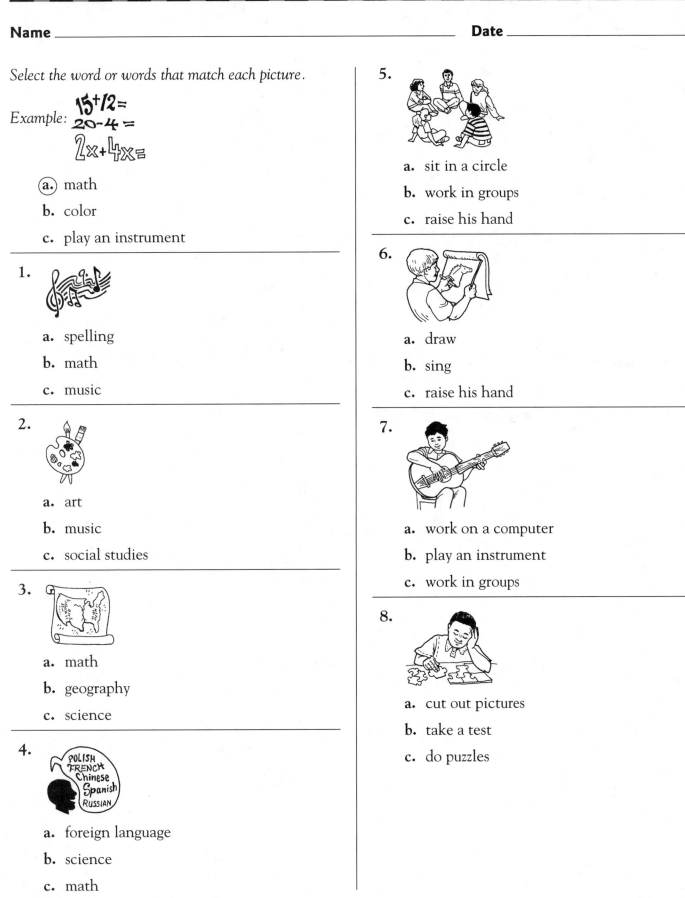

1.

a. spelling
b. math
c. music

2.

a. art
b. music
c. social studies

3.

a. math
b. geography
c. science

4. POLISH FRENCH Chinese Spanish RUSSIAN

a. foreign language
b. science
c. math

5.

a. sit in a circle
b. work in groups
c. raise his hand

6.

a. draw
b. sing
c. raise his hand

7.

a. work on a computer
b. play an instrument
c. work in groups

8.

a. cut out pictures
b. take a test
c. do puzzles

9.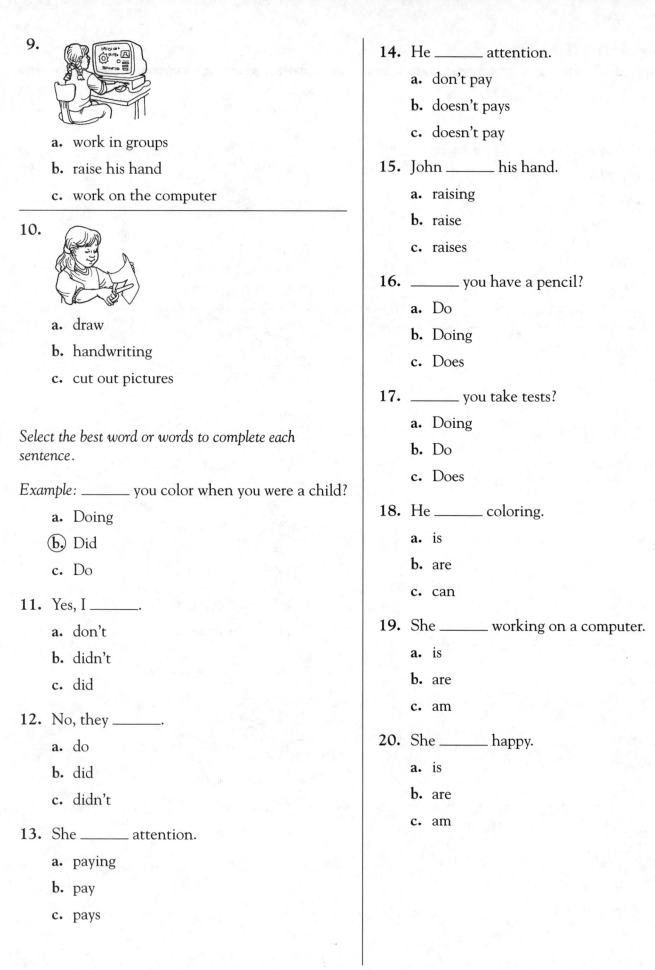

    a. work in groups

    b. raise his hand

    c. work on the computer

10.

    a. draw

    b. handwriting

    c. cut out pictures

Select the best word or words to complete each sentence.

Example: _____ you color when you were a child?

    a. Doing

    ⓑ Did

    c. Do

11. Yes, I _____.

    a. don't

    b. didn't

    c. did

12. No, they _____.

    a. do

    b. did

    c. didn't

13. She _____ attention.

    a. paying

    b. pay

    c. pays

14. He _____ attention.

    a. don't pay

    b. doesn't pays

    c. doesn't pay

15. John _____ his hand.

    a. raising

    b. raise

    c. raises

16. _____ you have a pencil?

    a. Do

    b. Doing

    c. Does

17. _____ you take tests?

    a. Doing

    b. Do

    c. Does

18. He _____ coloring.

    a. is

    b. are

    c. can

19. She _____ working on a computer.

    a. is

    b. are

    c. am

20. She _____ happy.

    a. is

    b. are

    c. am

Book 1

Book 1—Unit 1

Select the word that correctly completes each sentence.

Example: He _____ married.

    a. am

    b. are

    (**c.**) is

1. Her name _____ Mary.

    a. are

    b. is

    c. am

2. You _____ one child.

    a. is

    b. have

    c. has

3. _____ single.

    a. I is

    b. I are

    c. I am

4. Joe and Alice _____ married.

    a. are

    b. is

    c. be

5. We _____ from Texas.

    a. is

    b. are

    c. am

6. The United States _____ big.

    a. is

    b. am

    c. are

Choose the sentence that means the same.

Example: It is not quiet in the classroom.

    a. It's isn't quiet in the classroom.

    (**b.**) It's not quiet in the classroom.

    c. I'm not quiet in the classroom.

7. We are from Mexico.

    a. Were from Mexico.

    b. We're from Mexico.

    c. We'are from Mexico.

8. It is the same.

    a. It's the same.

    b. It'i the same.

    c. It i the same.

9. I am single.

    a. I'am single.

    b. Im single.

    c. I'm single.

10. They are in room 5.

    a. They'r in room 5.

    b. They're in room 5.

    a. The'yre in room 5.

11. I am not at work.

    a. I'm not at work.

    b. I'mn't at work.

    c. I amn't at work.

Choose the correct pronoun.

12. The book is on the table.

    a. He

    b. She

    c. It

13. Marc and Su-Jin are from Texas.

    a. He

    b. She

    c. They

14. John is married.

    a. He

    b. She

    c. It

15. Mary is at school.

    a. He

    b. She

    c. It

Look at the picture below. Answer the questions.

Example: Are the children at school?

    a. Yes, they are.

    b. Yes, they're not.

    c.) No, they're not.

16. Are José and Mariela married?

    a. Yes, they are.

    b. No, she isn't.

    c. No, he isn't.

17. Do they have three children?

    a. Yes, they do.

    b. No, they don't.

    c. Yes, she does.

18. Do they have a son?

    a. Yes, they don't.

    b. No, they do.

    c. Yes, they do.

Select the best answer for each question.

Example: What is your address?

    a.) 100 Ford Road

    b. Maria

    c. son

19. What is your name?

    a. Maria Gonzalez

    b. 97 East 9th Street

    c. New York City

20. What is your address?

    a. 17 Main Street

    b. Tommy Smith

    c. Russia

36

Book 1 — Unit 2

Name _____ Date _____

Select the opposite for each adjective.

Example: hot

    a. warm

    b. black

    (c.) old

1. expensive

    a. cheap

    b. poor

    c. rich

2. talkative

    a. noisy

    b. quiet

    c. lazy

3. dangerous

    a. hardworking

    b. nervous

    c. safe

4. nervous

    a. relaxed

    b. cheap

    c. quiet

5. hardworking

    a. lazy

    b. easy

    c. poor

Select an adjective that describes these things.

Example: The boy is _____.

    (a.) short

    b. opposite

    c. easy

6. The books are _____.

    a. hardworking

    b. easy

    c. nervous

7. My mother is _____.

    a. expensive

    b. east

    c. tall

8. It's here in the _____.

    a. north

    b. thirsty

    c. large

9. The classroom is _____.

    a. east

    b. noisy

    c. nervous

10. The man is _____.

    a. west

    b. new

    c. tired

Select the question that is written correctly.

Example:

    a. Am noisy I?

    b. Noisy am I?

    (c.) Am I noisy?

11. **a.** Street is your quiet?

    b. Is your street quiet?

    c. Your street quiet is?

12. **a.** Are you hardworking?

    b. Hardworking are you?

    c. You hardworking are?

13. **a.** It tall is?

    b. Tall is it?

    c. Is it tall?

14. **a.** She where is?

    b. Is where she?

    c. Where is she?

15. **a.** Is Russia a large country?

    b. Large country is Russia a?

    c. A large country is Russia?

Look at the picture below. Choose the correct answer.

Example: What's the name of the dog?

    a. Samby

    b. Debra

    (c.) Winston

16. What's the name of the city?

    a. Riga

    b. Boston

    c. New York

17. Is it hot today?

    a. Yes, it is.

    b. No, it is.

    c. No, it isn't.

18. Is Boston in the USA?

    a. Yes, it is.

    b. Yes, it isn't.

    c. No, it is.

19. Is the woman thirsty?

    a. Yes, she is.

    b. No, she isn't.

    c. No, she is.

20. Is the man busy?

    a. Yes, he is.

    b. No, he isn't.

    c. No, she isn't.

Boston
PUBLIC GARDEN
USA

Winston

Book 1—Unit 3

Select the words that go together.

Example:

    a. an dog

    (b.) a dog

1. **a.** a table
   b. an table

2. **a.** a umbrella
   b. an umbrella

3. **a.** a apple
   b. an apple

4. **a.** a American dictionary
   b. an American dictionary

5. **a.** a pencil sharpener
   b. an pencil sharpener

Decide whether each word is singular or plural.

Example: teacher

    (a.) singular

    b. plural

6. watches
   a. singular
   b. plural

7. people
   a. singular
   b. plural

8. clocks
   a. singular
   b. plural

9. women
   a. singular
   b. plural

10. dictionary
    a. singular
    b. plural

Select the time that matches the analog clock reading.

Example:

    (a.) five fifteen

    b. four forty-five

    c. four thirty-five

11.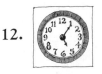
    a. six forty
    b. five twenty
    c. five forty

12.
    a. five oh-five
    b. four fifty-five
    c. five fifteen

13.
    a. five twenty-five
    b. five thirty-five
    c. five thirty

14.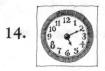

    a. four fifty

    b. five fifty

    c. five ten

15.

    a. three thirty

    b. three thirty-three

    c. three

Select the word that best completes each sentence.

Example: The store opens _____ 10:00.

    (**a.**) at

    b. in

    c. on

16. The class is _____ 9:00 to 10:00.

    a. at

    b. from

    c. on

17. I eat from 6:00 _____ 6:30 every evening.

    a. at

    b. from

    c. to

18. I work _____ 9:00 to 5:00.

    a. at

    b. from

    c. on

19. _____ are my books.

    a. These

    b. This

    c. That

20. _____ is my pen.

    a. These

    b. This

    c. Those

Book 1 — Unit 4

Fill in the blanks.

Example: _____ brother is married.

   a. Kathy

   b. She

   (**c.**) Kathy's

1. Rose is Mary's _____.

   a. grandmother

   b. grandparents

   c. children

2. Jane and Mark are Tommy's _____.

   a. mother

   b. father

   c. parents

3. Lilly is _____ sister.

   a. Amy

   b. Amy's

   c. she

4. This is _____ mother.

   a. an

   b. she

   c. my

5. There are _____ parents.

   a. a

   b. an

   c. her

6. Brian is _____ and John's brother.

   a. Millie's

   b. Millie

   c. She

7. _____ 19 years old.

   a. Terri

   b. Terri's

   c. Her's

8. _____ name is Donald.

   a. He

   b. He's

   c. His

9. _____ birthday is on August 4.

   a. She

   b. He

   c. His

10. _____ names are Jane and Kevin.

   a. They've

   b. Their

   c. Her

California
MOTOR VEHICLE SERVICES
LC697348215

SEX: M   HT.: 6'2"
EYES: BRN   DOB: 12-12-56
PHONE: 555-4506

ARTURO MENDOZA
117 PALMAS AVE.
SAN SIMEON, CA 94914

Arturo Mendoza

Answer these questions about the driver's license above.

Example: What's his first name?

   a. Mendoza

   b. Lopez

   (**c.**) Arturo

11. What's his last name?

  a. Mendoza

  b. Lopez

  c. Arturo

12. What's his address?

  a. 555-4506

  b. 117 Palmas Ave.

  c. LC697348215

13. What is his birth date?

  a. Dec. 12, 1956

  b. Dec. 2, 1956

  c. Nov. 12, 1956

14. What's his height?

  a. 2 feet, 6 inches

  b. 6 feet, 2 inches

  c. sixty-two inches

15. What color are his eyes?

  a. blue

  b. black

  c. brown

16. Elizabeth is Linda's _____.

  a. mother

  b. daughter

  c. brother

17. Linda is Howard's _____.

  a. mother

  b. daughter

  c. brother

18. Maria is Tom's _____.

  a. mother

  b. sister

  c. brother

19. Howard is Linda's _____.

  a. son

  b. daughter

  c. mother

20. Linda is Elizabeth's _____.

  a. mother

  b. daughter

  c. son

```
                 Elizabeth
                     |
                   Linda
                  /  |  \
          Howard   Maria   Tom
```

Choose the correct word to complete each sentence.

Example: Tom is Maria's _____.

  a. mother

  b. daughter

  (c.) brother

42

Name _____ **Date** _____

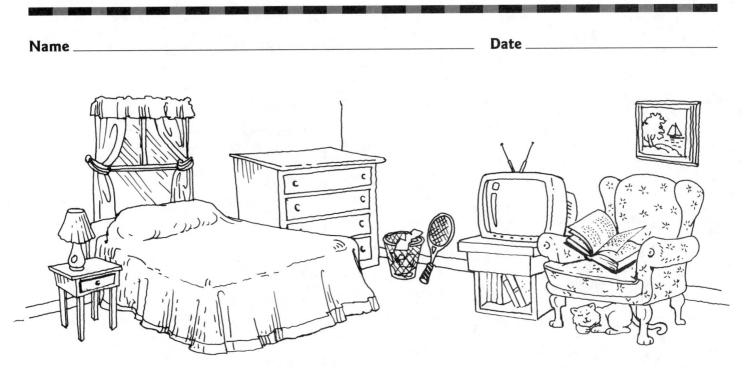

Choose the correct word or words to complete each sentence.

Example: The lamp is _____ the night table.

   (**a.**) on

   b. in

   c. under

1. The dresser is _____ the bed.

   a. on

   b. in

   c. next to

2. The window is _____ the bed.

   a. under

   b. over

   c. between

3. The tennis racquet is _____ the wastepaper basket.

   a. on

   b. in

   c. next to

4. The television is _____ the table.

   a. on

   b. in

   c. next to

5. The cat is _____ the chair.

   a. next to

   b. under

   c. on

6. The bed is _____ the dresser and the night table.

   a. between

   b. next to

   c. in

7. The book is _____ the chair.

   a. on

   b. in

   c. next to

8. The armchair is _____ the table.
   a. between
   b. next to
   c. over

9. The picture is _____ the chair.
   a. over
   b. on
   c. under

10. The night table is _____ the lamp.
    a. over
    b. on
    c. under

Choose the best answer.

Example: The refrigerator is in the _____.
   (a.) kitchen
   b. bedroom
   c. sink

11. The eggs are in the _____.
    a. refrigerator
    b. VCR
    c. coffee table

12. You cook with a _____.
    a. refrigerator
    b. map
    c. microwave

13. You talk on the _____.
    a. telephone
    b. fax machine
    c. calendar

14. You listen to the _____.
    a. desk
    b. chalkboard
    c. radio

15. You write on a _____.
    a. alarm clock
    b. chalkboard
    c. CD player

16. The toilet is in the _____.
    a. bathroom
    b. bedroom
    c. living room

17. The stove is in the _____.
    a. kitchen
    b. bedroom
    c. living room

18. A _____ tells time.
    a. stereo
    b. calendar
    c. clock

19. The shower is in the _____.
    a. kitchen
    b. living room
    c. bathroom

20. The dresser is in the _____.
    a. kitchen
    b. bathroom
    c. bedroom

Book 1 — Unit 6

Choose the best answer.

Example: The toy store is _____ River Road.

   (**a.**) on

   b. behind

   c. across from

1. The post office is _____ the diner.

   a. across from

   b. next to

   c. on

2. The supermarket is _____ Pine Avenue and Bay Street.

   a. on the corner of

   b. next to

   c. between

3. The jewelry store is _____ the drug store.

   a. on

   b. next to

   c. across from

4. The barber is _____ Second Street.

   a. on

   b. next to

   c. between

5. The drug store is _____ the jewelry store.

   a. next to

   b. between

   c. on

6. The toy store is _____ River Road.

   a. in

   b. next to

   c. on

7. The bank is _____ the diner on Center Street.

   a. between

   b. in

   c. next to

8. The diner is _____ the post office and the bank.

   a. on

   b. between

   c. next

9. The shoe store is _____ the Laundromat.

   a. on

   b. next

   c. next to

10. The shoe store is _____ the police station.

   a. between

   b. across

   c. across from

Choose the best answer.

Example: The Laundromat is _____ Lake Street.

    a. at

    b. on

    c. in

11. There is _____ on Central Avenue.

    a. an supermarket

    b. supermarket

    c. a supermarket

12. The fire station is _____ Highland Avenue.

    a. on

    b. in

    c. on the

13. _____ a car wash on Brook Street.

    a. They're

    b. There's

    c. There

14. It's _____ the corner of First Street and Pine Avenue.

    a. on

    b. in

    c. across

15. _____ Italian Restaurant?

    a. Where's

    b. Where's the

    c. Where

Choose the best answer.

Example: You can buy bread in a _____.

    a. bank

    b. bakery

    c. hospital

16. You get food in a _____.

    a. supermarket

    b. post office

    c. shoe store

17. You buy tickets in a _____.

    a. police station

    b. fire station

    c. bus station

18. You can find books in a _____.

    a. jewelry store

    b. diner

    c. library

19. You can wash your clothes at a _____.

    a. car wash

    b. Laundromat

    c. drug store

20. When you are very sick, you go to a _____.

    a. diner

    b. high school

    c. hospital

Choose the best word.

Example: Sam _____ a big dinner for his family.

  ⓐ **cooks**

  b. cook

  c. cooking

1. William _____ hot tea every evening.

  a. drink

  b. drinks

  c. drinking

2. They _____ at the diner on their way home from work.

  a. stop

  b. stops

  c. stopping

3. Lucy _____ a small cup of coffee for breakfast.

  a. have

  b. has

  c. having

4. Paul _____ lunch with his coworkers.

  a. eat

  b. eats

  c. eating

5. Joe and Betty _____ lunch in the cafeteria.

  a. don't buy

  b. doesn't buy

  c. do buys

6. She _____ at 6:00.

  a. got

  b. getting up

  c. gets up

7. My friend _____ me a ride.

  a. give

  b. gives

  c. giving

8. Tony _____ when it's raining.

  a. doesn't walk

  b. don't walking

  c. don't walks

9. Lucy goes to English class _____ Monday nights.

  a. on

  b. at

  c. in

10. I do my homework _____ the evenings.

  a. on

  b. at

  c. in

11. I relax _____ the weekend.

  a. on

  b. at

  c. in

12. I sleep _____ 10:00 to 6:00.

  a. on

  b. from

  c. at

13. I go to work _____ 10:00.

    a. on

    b. from

    c. at

14. I take walks _____ the summer.

    a. in

    b. on

    c. at

15. I eat Mexican food _____.

    a. once in week

    b. once on week

    c. once a week

16. They get paid _____ Thursdays.

    a. in

    b. on

    c. at

17. Millie cooks _____ a day.

    a. once times

    b. twice times

    c. three times

18. She exercises _____.

    a. day every

    b. day time every

    c. every day

19. When he's cold, he _____ a bath.

    a. take

    b. doesn't take

    c. don't take

20. When they're bored, they _____ a book.

    a. read

    b. reads

    c. reading

Book 1 — Unit 8

Name _____ Date _____

Choose the best answer.

Example: Do you work full time?

(a.) Yes, I do.

b. Yes, I does.

c. Yes, I doing.

1. Do you speak Spanish at work?

   a. Yes, I do.

   b. Yes, I don't.

   c. No, I do.

2. Do they work hard?

   a. Yes, they don't.

   b. No, they don't.

   c. No, they doesn't.

3. Is her job boring?

   a. Yes, it aren't.

   b. Yes, it are.

   c. Yes, it is.

4. Do we work with children?

   a. No, we do.

   b. No, we don't.

   c. Yes, we does.

5. Does she use cash?

   a. Yes, she do.

   b. No, she don't.

   c. Yes, she does.

6. Does he work part time?

   a. No, he don't.

   b. No, he do.

   c. No, he doesn't.

7. Do you help people?

   a. Yes, I does.

   b. Yes, I do.

   c. No, I doesn't.

8. Is your job messy?

   a. No, it is.

   b. No it aren't.

   c. No, it isn't.

9. Does it help?

   a. Yes, it don't.

   b. No, it doesn't.

   c. No, it does.

10. Does she work at the bakery?

    a. Yes, she do.

    b. Yes, she does.

    c. No, she does.

11. Who works part time?

    a. Bill and Mary doesn't.

    b. Bill and Mary isn't.

    c. Bill and Mary do.

12. Where does he work?

    a. He's work at the restaurant.

    b. He works at the restaurant.

    c. He work at the restaurant.

13. Where does she work?

    a. She works at the store.

    b. She work at the store.

    c. She working at the store.

14. When do they work?

   a. They work from 8:00 to 5:00.

   b. They works from 8:00 to 5:00.

   c. They working from 8:00 to 5:00.

15. What hours does Jim work?

   a. He works from 2:00 to 10:00.

   b. He working from 2:00 to 10:00.

   c. He work from 2:00 to 10:00.

Look at the picture. Choose the best answer.

Example: Does she look at driver's licenses?

   a. No, she doesn't.

   (b.) Yes, she does.

   c. No, she does.

16. Does she work inside?

   a. Yes, she does.

   b. I don't know.

   c. No, she doesn't.

17. Does she wear a uniform?

   a. I don't know.

   b. No, she doesn't.

   c. Yes, she does.

18. Does she speak English at work?

   a. Yes, she does.

   b. No, she doesn't.

   c. No, she speaks Chinese.

19. Where is she working today?

   a. She is working at the corner of Main and Fourth Streets.

   b. She is working in a school.

   c. She is working in a police car.

20. Does she stand at work?

   a. No, she doesn't.

   b. Yes, she does.

   c. I don't know.

50

Choose the correct sentence.

Example:

   (a.) There is a banana.

   b. There is an banana.

   c. There are some banana.

1. a. There is a ketchup.
   b. There is an ketchup.
   c. There is some ketchup.

2. a. There is a apple.
   b. There is an apple.
   c. There are some apple.

3. a. There is a soy sauce.
   b. There is an soy sauce.
   c. There is some soy sauce.

4. a. There is a broccoli.
   b. There is an broccoli.
   c. There is some broccoli.

5. a. There is a tissue.
   b. There is an tissue.
   c. There are some tissue.

6. a. There is a onions.
   b. There is an onions.
   c. There are some onions.

7. a. There is a orange.
   b. There is an orange.
   c. There are some orange.

8. a. There is a bread.
   b. There is an bread.
   c. There is some bread.

9. a. There is a butter.
   b. There is an butter.
   c. There is some butter.

10. a. There are some rice in the cabinet.
    b. There is some rice in the cabinet.
    c. There is a rice in the cabinet.

11. a. There is a milk in the refrigerator.
    b. There are a milk in the refrigerator.
    c. There is some milk in the refrigerator.

12. a. There is some chicken on the stove.
    b. There are some chicken on the stove.
    c. There is an chicken on the stove.

13. a. There is a spaghetti in the cabinet.
    b. There are a spaghetti in the cabinet.
    c. There is some spaghetti in the cabinet.

14. a. There are vegetables on the counter.
    b. There is vegetable on the counter.
    c. There is a vegetables on the counter.

15. a. There is a pretzel in the bag.
    b. There are a pretzels in the bag.
    c. There is pretzel in the bag.

16. **a.** There are a box of cookies in the cabinet.

    b. There is some box of cookies in the cabinet.

    c. There is a box of cookies in the cabinet.

17. **a.** There is can of soup in the cabinet.

    b. There is some can of soup in the cabinet.

    c. There is a can of soup in the cabinet.

18. **a.** There is a bottle of soda in the refrigerator.

    b. There is bottle of soda in the refrigerator.

    c. There is some bottle of soda in the refrigerator.

19. **a.** There is an Italian dressing the bottle.

    b. There are Italian dressing in the bottle.

    c. There is some Italian dressing in the bottle.

20. **a.** There is a jelly in the jar.

    b. There is some jelly in the jar.

    c. There are jelly in the jar.

Book 1 — Unit 10

Name _____   Date _____

Choose the best response.

Example: Carlos _____ in the kitchen.

    a. sit

    (b.) is sitting

    c. are sitting

1. Mary _____ a pretty skirt.

    a. wear

    b. wearing

    c. is wearing

2. Carl and Marcos _____ books.

    a. reads

    b. are reading

    c. is reading

3. No one _____ on the chair.

    a. sit

    b. sitting

    c. is sitting

4. She _____ her pencil.

    a. sharpen

    b. is sharpening

    c. sharpening

5. He _____ talking.

    a. is

    b. are

    c. am

6. She _____ letters every day.

    a. write

    b. writes

    c. writing

7. They _____ three times a day.

    a. eat

    b. eats

    c. eating

8. Joe _____ to the teacher.

    a. listen

    b. listening

    c. listens

9. Rita _____ writing on the board.

    a. are

    b. aren't

    c. isn't

10. Joe and Ellen _____ speaking English.

    a. is

    b. not

    c. aren't

11. Linda _____ writing to her mother.

    a. are

    b. is

    c. not

12. The teachers _____ teaching today.

    a. are

    b. is

    c. not

13. _____ drinking coffee.

    a. They

    b. They're not

    c. They is not

14. I _____ her mother every day.

   a. call

   b. not call

   c. calls

15. I _____ working today.

   a. is

   b. is not

   c. am

Indicate if the action is present continuous (now) or routine.

Example: My mother cooks three times a day.

   a. now

   (b.) routine

16. Jill and Jack are walking up the hill.

   a. now

   b. routine

17. Mary stands at the bus stop every day.

   a. now

   b. routine

18. I am writing a letter.

   a. now

   b. routine

19. She drinks a lot of coffee.

   a. now

   b. routine

20. We are studying.

   a. now

   b. routine

Choose the correct sentence or phrase.

Example:

    (a.) Are Mary and Lisa paying?

    b. Are she paying?

    c. Are I paying?

1. What is she ordering?

    a. She ordering coffee.

    b. She is ordering coffee.

    c. She's order lunch.

2. **a.** Is she drives a car?

    b. Is she driving a car?

    c. Is she drive a car?

3. **a.** Are she waiting?

    b. Is they waiting?

    c. Is he waiting?

4. **a.** Is it cooking?

    b. Are it cooking?

    c. Is it cook?

5. **a.** Are cooking?

    b. Are they cooking?

    c. Is they cooking?

6. **a.** Are he drinking a soda?

    b. Is you drinking a soda?

    c. Is he drinking a soda?

7. **a.** What am you ordering?

    b. What is I ordering?

    c. What are you ordering?

8. **a.** Why am I eating?

    b. Why is I eating?

    c. Why are I eating?

9. **a.** Why she is eating?

    b. Why is she eating?

    c. Why she are eating?

10. **a.** Where you are walking?

    b. Where is you walking?

    c. Where are you walking?

11. **a.** No, it isn't.

    b. No, it are.

    c. No, it aren't.

12. **a.** Yes, it isn't.

    b. Yes, you aren't.

    c. No, you aren't.

13. Is she wearing a uniform?

    a. Yes, she is.

    b. Yes, she isn't.

    c. Yes, it is.

14. Are they waiting inside the car?

    a. Yes, they are.

    b. Yes, they aren't.

    c. No, they is.

15. Are they eating hamburgers?

    a. Yes, she is.

    b. Yes, they are.

    c. No, he isn't.

16. What is she eating?

    a. A hamburger.

    b. A table.

    c. A soda.

17. When is he working?

    a. Today, from 1:00 to 5:00.

    b. At a restaurant.

    c. Because he's hungry.

18. Why are they drinking?

    a. Because they're ordering.

    b. Inside a restaurant.

    c. Because they're thirsty.

19. Where are you walking?

    a. Drive.

    b. From 1:00 to 2:00.

    c. To a restaurant.

20. Who is she paying?

    a. The cashier.

    b. The soccer game.

    c. The car.

Book 1 — Unit 12

Choose the best word or words.

Example: There _____ five garbage cans.

    a. is

    (b.) are

    c. isn't

1. There _____ cars outside.

    a. are any

    b. aren't any

    c. is any

2. There _____ bus stop on the corner.

    a. is some

    b. is a

    c. a few

3. There _____ students in the parking lot.

    a. is a

    b. are a

    c. are some

4. There _____ pay telephone inside.

    a. is a

    b. are a

    c. are some

5. There _____ dogs outside.

    a. is many

    b. is some

    c. are many

6. _____ hungry.

    a. They are

    b. There are

    c. There is

7. _____ a statue inside the building.

    a. There are

    b. They are

    c. There is

8. _____ a student parking lot.

    a. It's

    b. There are

    c. They are

9. _____ are late.

    a. There

    b. It

    c. They

10. _____ tall.

    a. There is

    b. It is

    c. They is

11. _____ there books on the shelf?

    a. Is

    b. Isn't

    c. Are

12. Is there _____ rice?

    a. a

    b. any

    c. an

13. Is there a parking lot?
No, there _____.

    a. isn't

    b. aren't

    c. is

14. Are there fax machines in the office?

    a. No, there is one.

    b. Yes, there are many.

    c. No, there are a fax machine.

15. Is there a security booth inside?

    a. Yes, there is some.

    b. Yes, there is many.

    c. Yes, there is one.

Choose the sentence with the correct word order.

Example:

    a. Any machines fax in office your are there?

    b. Fax machines in your office any are there?

    (c.) Are there any fax machines in your office?

16. **a.** Are there any holidays in November?

    b. Are any there holidays in November?

    c. There are any holidays in November?

17. **a.** How many elevators there are?

    b. There are elevators, how many?

    c. How many elevators are there?

18. **a.** Are there mailboxes some?

    b. Some mailboxes are there?

    c. Are there some mailboxes?

19. **a.** There is any school on Independence Day?

    b. Is there any school on Independence Day?

    c. Is any there school on Independence Day?

20. **a.** Is there a water fountain near the building?

    b. Near the building a water fountain is there?

    c. There is a water fountain near the building?

Book 1 — Unit 13

Choose the best response for each question.

Example: Can she write her name?

   a. Yes, she can't.

   b. No, she can.

   c. Yes, she can.

1. What's the weather like in Alaska?

   a. It's cloudy.

   b. Yes, it is.

   c. It's 250 degrees.

2. What's the temperature in Chicago?

   a. It's 22 degrees.

   b. No, it isn't.

   c. It's foggy.

3. What part of the country do you live in?

   a. The fog.

   b. The southwest.

   c. Very cold.

4. How many seasons are there?

   a. two

   b. four

   c. one

5. Can she play tennis?

   a. Yes, she can.

   b. Yes, she can't.

   c. No, he can.

6. Can your brother ski?

   a. Yes, he can't.

   b. Yes, she can.

   c. Yes, he can.

7. Can Sam and Mary play tennis?

   a. Yes, she can.

   b. Yes, she can't.

   c. Yes, they can.

8. Can we surf?

   a. No, you can.

   b. No, you can't.

   c. Yes, you can't.

9. Can you sail?

   a. Yes, I can't.

   b. Yes, she can.

   c. No, I can't.

10. Can your teacher swim?

   a. Yes, they can.

   b. Yes, we can.

   c. Yes, she can.

Look at the pictures above. Answer the questions.

Example: Is it hot?

   a. Yes, it isn't.

   b. No, it isn't.

   c. Yes, it is.

11. Can she roller skate?

   a. No, she can.

   b. No, she can't.

   c. Yes, she can't.

12. Can he play baseball?

   a. Yes, he can.

   b. No, he can't.

   c. Yes, she can.

13. Is it foggy?

   a. No, it isn't.

   b. No, it can't.

   c. Yes, it is.

14. What is he wearing?

   a. A dress.

   b. A baseball cap.

   c. A coat.

Use the information in the letter to answer the questions.

15. Is it raining?

   a. Yes, it is.

   b. No, it is.

   c. No, it isn't.

16. Is it hot?

   a. No, it is.

   b. Yes, it is.

   c. No, it isn't.

17. Is it snowing?

   a. No, it isn't.

   b. Yes, it is.

   c. No, it can't.

Dear Grandma,

I am having fun in Orlando, Florida.

Today it is a hot and sunny, 92 degrees.

I like to sail with my friends. I am happy because I can swim.

Love, Marc

Age 8

18. Can Marc swim?

   a. Yes, he can swim.

   b. No, they can't.

   c. No, he can't.

19. What's the temperature in Orlando, Florida?

   a. 92 degrees

   b. 29 degrees

   c. 48 degrees

20. What can he do outside?

   a. snow ski

   b. ice skate

   c. sail

Book 1 — Unit 14

Name _____ **Date** _____

Select the best word to complete each sentence.

Example: _____ Atlanta, the weather is cloudy.

   (**a.**) In

   b. On

   c. At

1. How was the weather _____ Chicago?

   a. in

   b. on

   c. at

2. How _____ the weather in Florida?

   a. was

   b. were

   c. are

3. The room _____ small.

   a. was

   b. were

   c. are

4. The towels _____ clean.

   a. was

   b. were

   c. is

5. The food _____ terrible.

   a. was

   b. were

   c. are

6. _____ was the beach in California?

   a. They

   b. When

   c. How

7. _____ the food expensive?

   a. When

   b. Was

   c. How

8. _____ the waiters friendly?

   a. Were

   b. Is

   c. Was

9. The woman _____ happy.

   a. were

   b. are

   c. was

10. At Lupie's Restaurant, _____ the food spicy?

   a. were

   b. was

   c. are

*Find the best **question** for each **answer**.*

Example: Yes, it was.

   (**a.**) Was it uncomfortable?

   b. Were they uncomfortable?

   c. Weren't they uncomfortable?

11. The room was large.

   a. Where was the room?

   b. How was the room in Miami?

   c. Why was the room in Miami?

12. No, they weren't.
    a. Who were Chris and Tom?
    b. Were Chris and Tom friendly?
    c. Where were Chris and Tom?

13. It was near the beach.
    a. Where was the restaurant?
    b. How was the restaurant?
    c. How was the beach?

14. No, it was quiet.
    a. Were they noisy?
    b. Was it friendly?
    c. Was it noisy?

15. I ate there last week.
    a. Where did you eat?
    b. Was the dinner tasty?
    c. When was the last time you ate there?

16. She was in China.
    a. Where was the woman?
    b. Was it large?
    c. When were you there?

17. James Stewart.
    a. Who was a famous actor?
    b. Was he friendly?
    c. How was the man?

18. No, the men were old.
    a. Were the men young?
    b. Were they friendly?
    c. Were they upset?

19. It was warm and sunny.
    a. How was the motel?
    b. Was it old?
    c. How was the weather in Hawaii?

20. It was a party.
    a. Who was there?
    b. Where was it?
    c. What was the occasion?

Book 1 — Unit 15

Select the correct word or words to complete the sentence.

Example: She _____ for a job.

   a. applieded

   b. applied

   c. appliete

1. Jushi _____ sick.

   a. felt

   b. feeled

   c. feel

2. Mariela _____ at the new car for an hour.

   a. locked

   b. looked

   c. lookt

3. Tomas _____ a watch.

   a. find

   b. founded

   c. found

4. She _____ $115.00 in the bank.

   a. depaisit

   b. deposited

   c. deposit

5. I _____ a letter.

   a. mauled

   b. mailed

   c. maild

6. We _____ new cameras.

   a. got

   b. gets

   c. gotted

7. You _____ an old pair of shoes.

   a. has

   b. had

   c. haved

8. They _____ for the car.

   a. wait

   b. waited

   c. waiteded

9. He _____ lunch.

   a. enjoyed

   b. enjoy

   c. enjouyete

10. My mother _____ late.

   a. sleep

   b. sleeped

   c. slept

11. Last Monday, my father _____ to the barbershop.

   a. goed

   b. goes

   c. went

12. My relatives _____ us last month.

   a. does visit

   b. didn't visit

   c. did visits

13. Yesterday, I _____ sleep late.

   a. did no

   b. don't

   c. didn't

14. _____ he work last week?

   a. Did

   b. Do

   c. Does

15. _____ you just buy your books 5 minutes ago?

   a. Didn't

   b. Don't

   c. Doesn't

16. Did I smile?
Yes, you _____.

   a. do

   b. doesn't

   c. did

17. Did they arrive early?
No, they _____.

   a. didn't

   b. doesn't

   c. don't

18. _____ it snow last year?

   a. Do

   b. Does

   c. Did

19. _____ I pay my bill two days ago?

   a. Don't

   b. Doesn't

   c. Didn't

20. Did you go to the movies last week?
No, we _____.

   a. don't

   b. didn't

   c. doesn't

Book 1—Unit 16

Name _____   **Date** _____

Select the correct word to complete each sentence.

Example: I _____ from high school last year.

   a. graduate

   b. graduates

   (**c.**) graduated

1. Yesterday morning, she _____ school.

   a. starts

   b. started

   c. start

2. Last year, he _____ in love.

   a. fall

   b. fell

   c. falled

3. They _____ the soccer game.

   a. wins

   b. win

   c. won

4. Mrs. Davis _____ school in Africa in 1975.

   a. taught

   b. teach

   c. teached

5. She _____ the answers.

   a. knew

   b. know

   c. knowing

Select the question that is worded correctly.

Example:

   a. When child yours was born?

   (**b.**) When was your child born?

   c. Your child born was when?

6. **a.** Alone did you go to the movies?

   b. Did you go to the movies alone?

   c. Go to the movies alone, did you?

7. **a.** Read, who taught you how to?

   b. How to read who taught you?

   c. Who taught you how to read?

8. **a.** Why did she move to North Carolina?

   b. She did move why to North Carolina?

   c. North Carolina, why did she move to?

9. **a.** Where her first job was?

   b. Where was her first job?

   c. Her first job where was?

10. **a.** Graduate from where did they?

   b. They graduate did from where?

   c. Where did they graduate from?

*Select the best **question** for each **answer**.*

Example: Yes, it did.

   (**a.**) Did it rain?

   b. Don't it rain?

   c. Can't it rain?

11. To visit Mrs. Pennell.

   a. When did she come?

   b. Why did she come?

   c. How did she come?

12. By boat.

   a. How did they come?

   b. When did they come?

   c. Why did they come?

13. From January to June.

   a. How long did they stay?

   b. Where did they go?

   c. When did they come?

14. Yes, he did.

   a. Did she come alone?

   b. Did he come alone?

   c. Did his come alone?

15. Harvard University.

   a. Where did Dr. Hafler graduate from?

   b. Why did Dr. Hafler graduate?

   c. When did Dr. Hafler graduate?

16. Because she liked Chinese food.

   a. Why did she go to the Chinese restaurant?

   b. Where did she go?

   c. Why did she go to the Mexican restaurant?

17. Beans and rice.

   a. Where did you eat?

   b. Why did you eat?

   c. What did you eat?

18. Six years.

   a. Why did you study?

   b. When did you study?

   c. How long did you study English?

19. José and Marta.

   a. Who stayed home from school?

   b. Did they stay home from school?

   c. Why did they stay home from school?

20. In 1977.

   a. Why did you get your first job?

   b. When did you get your first job?

   c. Where did you get your first job?

Book 1—Unit 17

Name _____ **Date** _____

Read each sentence. If it describes right now, mark **now**. _If it describes the future, mark_ **future**.

Example: She is watching a movie.

   (**a.**) now

   b. future

1. I am going to study English.

   a. now

   b. future

2. Julia is reading her book.

   a. now

   b. future

3. They're walking on the beach.

   a. now

   b. future

4. I'm opening my mail.

   a. now

   b. future

5. You're going to arrive at 6:00.

   a. now

   b. future

Select the best word or words to complete each sentence.

Example: She _____ finishing her homework.

   (**a.**) is

   b. are

   c. going

6. I _____ going to study.

   a. are

   b. am

   c. is

7. We _____ going to buy our boots.

   a. are

   b. am

   c. is

8. I'm _____ clean the living room.

   a. going

   b. to

   c. going to

9. She _____ setting the table.

   a. is

   b. is going to

   c. is going

10. _____ hanging up the coats.

   a. They's

   b. They're

   c. They

11. _____ is going to clean the house?

   a. Who

   b. Why

   c. How

12. _____ is going to the movies?

   a. Who

   b. Why

   c. How

13. I _____ to work.

   a. is going

   b. are going

   c. am going

14. They _____ to sleep.

   a. is going

   b. are going

   c. am going

15. He _____ to eat.

   a. is going

   b. are going

   c. am going

16. We _____ to set the tables.

   a. is going

   b. are going

   c. am going

17. I _____ going to wash the dishes.

   a. am not

   b. are not

   c. is not

18. He _____ to vacuum the carpet.

   a. am not

   b. are not

   c. is not

19. You _____ to fix the car.

   a. am not

   b. are not

   c. is not

20. They _____ going to the party.

   a. am not

   b. are not

   c. is not

Book 1 — Unit 18

Name _____   Date _____

Select the best word or words to complete each sentence.

Example: _____ I going to see you?

    a. Are

    (b.) Am

    c. Is

1. _____ you going to Germany?

    a. Are

    b. Am

    c. Is

2. _____ it going to rain?

    a. Are

    b. Am

    c. Is

3. we going to eat Mexican food?

    a. Are

    b. Am

    c. Is

4. _____ she going to be our teacher?

    a. Are

    b. Am

    c. Is

5. _____ you going to eat supper?

    a. Are

    b. Am

    c. Is

6. _____ he going to pay the check?

    a. Are

    b. Am

    c. Is

7. _____ I going to fly?

    a. Are

    b. Am

    c. Is

8. _____ long are they going to stay?

    a. When

    b. What

    c. How

9. When _____ it going to arrive?

    a. are

    b. am

    c. is

10. Where _____ we going to go?

    a. are

    b. am

    c. is

11. _____ is it going to leave?

    a. When

    b. What

    c. Long how

12. Yes, you _____.

   a. are

   b. aren't

   c. is

13. No, you _____.

   a. isn't

   b. aren't

   c. am not

14. No, I _____.

   a. isn't

   b. aren't

   c. am not

15. No, they _____.

   a. isn't

   b. aren't

   c. am not

16. No, we _____.

   a. isn't

   b. aren't

   c. am not

17. No, it _____.

   a. isn't

   b. aren't

   c. am not

18. Yes, we _____.

   a. are

   b. am

   c. is

19. Yes, it _____.

   a. are

   b. am

   c. is

20. Yes, I _____.

   a. are

   b. am

   c. is

Book 2—Unit 1

Name _____ **Date** _____

Look at the picture of Arturo.

Example: Arturo _____ a computer programmer.

   (**a.**) is

   b. isn't

   c. are

1. He _____ a police officer.

   a. is

   b. are

   c. isn't

2. There _____ pictures on his computer.

   a. is

   b. are

   c. aren't

3. The work _____ interesting.

   a. are

   b. is

   c. aren't

4. His hours _____ terrible.

   a. are

   b. is

   c. isn't

5. His work _____ in his home.

   a. are

   b. is

   c. aren't

Select the contraction that matches the words listed.

Example: I am =

   a. I'am

   (**b.**) I'm

   c. Im'

6. you are =

   a. you'are

   b. you're

   c. you'a

7. it is =

   a. 'tis

   b. It'is

   c. It's

8. is not =

   a. is'not

   b. isn't

   c. ins't

9. are not =

   a. rn't

   b. ren't

   c. aren't

10. he is =

   a. he's

   b. hese

   c. she's

Select the best answer for each question.

Example: Is that the Trade Tower?

    a. Yes, I am.

    (b.) No, it isn't.

    c. Yes, it isn't.

11. Are you at work?

    a. Yes, I are.

    b. No, I am.

    c. Yes, I am.

12. Is she in the office?

    a. No, she is.

    b. No, she isn't.

    c. Yes, she are.

13. Are the optometrists in their offices?

    a. Yes, they aren't

    b. Yes, they are.

    c. Yes, they am.

14. Are we home yet?

    a. Yes, we aren't.

    b. No, we are.

    c. No, we aren't.

15. Are you on Las Fuentas Drive?

    a. Yes, I are.

    b. Yes, I is.

    c. Yes, I am.

16. Mary works _____ Atlanta.

    a. at

    b. in

    c. on

17. Tommy isn't _____ school today.

    a. at

    b. is

    c. on

18. Laura's office is _____ the seventh floor.

    a. at

    b. in

    c. on

19. Mildred works _____ a law office.

    a. at

    b. in

    c. on

20. The doctors are _____ a meeting.

    a. at

    b. in

    c. on

Book 2—Unit 2

Fill in each blank with the correct word or phrase.

Example: I _____ to eat pizza two times a week.

   ⓐ like

   b. doesn't like

   c. don't likes

1. She _____ long hours.

   a. work

   b. doesn't work

   c. don't works

2. Mr. and Mrs. Jones _____ typical Italians.

   a. are no

   b. are not

   c. is not

3. He _____ wash the dishes.

   a. do

   b. don't

   c. doesn't

4. They _____ in June.

   a. graduates

   b. graduate

   c. graduating

5. She _____ milk every morning.

   a. dranked

   b. drinketh

   c. drinks

6. They _____ health insurance.

   a. receive

   b. receiver

   c. receiving

7. I only _____ on Mondays and Tuesdays.

   a. works

   b. work

   c. working

8. It _____ with coffee and dessert.

   a. comes

   b. come

   c. coming

9. We _____ because we have a car.

   a. don't walk

   b. doesn't walk

   c. walks

10. The average student _____ enough.

   a. don't study

   b. study

   c. doesn't study

11. I _____ two brothers and three sisters.

   a. haves

   b. has

   c. have

12. They _____ a dog.

   a. don't has

   b. don't have

   c. doesn't have

13. I know a person who _____ like cars.

   a. don't

   b. doezn't

   c. doesn't

14. I _____ to school everyday.

    a. goes

    b. goez

    c. go

15. Mark _____ to work by bus.

    a. goes

    b. goez

    c. go

16. Most children _____ to school.

    a. goez

    b. goes

    c. go

17. Mary _____ an excellent teacher.

    a. is

    b. aren't

    c. are

18. We _____ work on Saturdays.

    a. does

    b. don't

    c. doesn't

19. Every year, we _____ 1000 answering machines.

    a. fix

    b. fixes

    c. fixing

20. Some people _____ twelve hours of television a day.

    a. watches

    b. watch

    c. watching

Book 2—Unit 3

Name _____ Date _____

Choose the correct word to complete each sentence.

Example: Yes, it _____.

   (a.) does

   b. do

   c. don't

1. Yes, she _____.

   a. do

   b. does

   c. don't

2. Yes, I _____.

   a. do

   b. does

   c. don't

3. Yes, we _____.

   a. do

   b. does

   c. don't

4. Yes, they _____.

   a. does

   b. do

   c. don't

5. Yes, you _____.

   a. does

   b. do

   c. don't

6. No, I _____.

   a. doesn't

   b. do

   c. don't

7. No, he _____.

   a. doesn't

   b. do

   c. don't

8. No, they _____.

   a. doesn't

   b. do

   c. don't

9. No, it _____.

   a. doesn't

   b. do

   c. don't

10. _____ I teach?

   a. Does

   b. Do

   c. Doesn't

11. _____ she study hard?

   a. Does

   b. Do

   c. Don't

12. When _____ you walk?

   a. do

   b. does

   c. don't

13. How long _____ it take?

   a. do

   b. does

   c. don't

14. Where _____ they live?

    a. don't

    b. do

    c. does

15. When _____ she sleep?

    a. does

    b. do

    c. don't

Select the word or words that best answer the question.

16. Where do they go to school?

    a. In Concord, California

    b. On California

    c. At Concord, California

17. How do you travel to work?

    a. In car

    b. At car

    c. By car

18. How long does the train take?

    a. An hour

    b. By hour

    c. In hour

19. When does the plane arrive?

    a. On 3:00

    b. In 3:00

    c. At 3:00

20. How often do you drive to school?

    a. Rarely

    b. On time

    c. At time

Name _____ **Date** _____

Fill in the blank with the word that best completes each sentence.

Example: The plateau in Arizona _____ home to many Native Americans.

   a. are

   (b.) is

   c. were

1. The climate _____ very pleasant in Hawaii.

   a. is

   b. are

   c. were

2. Major earthquakes _____ very frightening.

   a. is

   b. are

   c. was

3. The cave _____ near the ocean.

   a. is

   b. are

   c. were

4. The students _____ to Mexico every summer.

   a. traveling

   b. travel

   c. travels

5. The traffic _____ very slowly.

   a. moving

   b. move

   c. moves

6. There _____ many students in my afternoon class.

   a. is

   b. are

7. There _____ a lot of snow.

   a. is

   b. are

8. There _____ a few workers in the cafeteria.

   a. is

   b. are

9. There _____ a little tourism in the mountain village.

   a. is

   b. are

10. There _____ one large lake.

   a. is

   b. are

11. How _____ sunshine is there in New York?

   a. many

   b. much

12. How _____ crime is there in Los Angeles?

   a. many

   b. much

13. How _____ volcanoes are there in Hawaii?

   a. many

   b. much

14. How _____ fishing is there in Hawaii?

   a. many

   b. much

15. How _____ swamps are there in Florida?

   a. many

   b. much

Choose the plural that is spelled correctly.

Example:

   a. farm

   (b.) farms

   c. farmes

16. **a.** classes

   b. class

   c. classs

17. **a.** industry

   b. industries

   c. industrys

18. **a.** man

   b. mans

   c. men

19. **a.** peoples

   b. person

   c. people

20. **a.** children

   b. childs

   c. childrens

Book 2—Unit 5

Name _____   **Date** _____

Select the best word or words to complete each sentence.

Example: I _____ listening to the teacher.

   (**a.**) am

   b. is

   c. are

1. He _____ eating breakfast.

   a. am

   b. is

   c. are

2. We _____ waiting for my husband.

   a. am

   b. is

   c. are

3. The plane _____ leaving.

   a. am

   b. is

   c. are

4. _____ Mary eating?

   a. Am

   b. Is

   c. Are

5. _____, she is.

   a. Yes

   b. No

6. _____, it isn't.

   a. Yes

   b. No

7. _____, they aren't.

   a. Yes

   b. No

8. _____, they are.

   a. Yes

   b. No

9. _____ Tom and Gail watching a movie?

   a. Are

   b. Is

   c. What

10. _____ large is the school?

   a. Where

   b. How

   c. What

11. Right now, Lucy _____ a train for Chicago.

   a. is boarding

   b. is boards

   c. boards

12. Tommy _____ anything the teacher is saying.

   a. don't understand

   b. don't understanding

   c. doesn't understand

13. The orange _____ sweet.

   a. tastes

   b. is tasting

   c. tasting

14. _____ is Flight 66 landing?

    a. What

    b. Which

    c. When

15. Teresa _____ her suitcase.

    a. is pulling

    b. is handing

    c. is landing

Select the best question to match the answer.

Example: Answer: At 9:30.

    a. What are they doing?

    (b.) When are they arriving?

    c. Why are they leaving?

16. Answer: Eating dinner.

    a. When are they eating?

    b. What are they doing?

    c. Where are they eating?

17. Answer: To Rome.

    a. When are we going?

    b. Why are we going?

    c. Where are we going?

18. Answer: In an hour.

    a. Where is she going?

    b. When is she leaving?

    c. Why is she leaving?

19. Answer: A newspaper.

    a. Why is he reading?

    b. When is he reading?

    c. What is he reading?

20. Answer: A salad.

    a. What are you drinking?

    b. When are you eating?

    c. What are you eating?

Book 2—Unit 6

Choose the answer that describes the group of words.

Example: Pizza, hamburger, chicken, salad

    a. work

    (b.) food

    c. flowers

1. Texas, Alaska, California, Nevada

    a. cities

    b. states

    c. countries

2. Clinton, Lincoln, Washington, Kennedy

    a. presidents

    b. flowers

    c. flags

3. cookies, cake, brownies, apple pie

    a. vegetables

    b. fruit

    c. desserts

4. dogs, cats, goldfish, hamsters

    a. pets

    b. colors

    c. breads

5. Boston, San Francisco, Chicago, London

    a. clothes

    b. cities

    c. countries

Pick the best word or words to complete each sentence.

Example: Alex _____ glasses.

    a. wearing

    (b.) wears

    c. wear

6. No one _____ any money.

    a. having

    b. have

    c. has

7. None of us _____ the train to work.

    a. take

    b. taking

    c. takes

8. _____ anyone absent today?

    a. Are

    b. Can

    c. Is

9. _____ all of your teachers from England?

    a. Are

    b. Can

    c. Is

10. _____ all of the females have short hair?

    a. Do

    b. Does

    c. Is

11. Cindy and Paul _____ all of the time.

    a. working

    b. works

    c. work

12. _____ all the children at the party?

    a. Was

    b. Were

    c. Is

13. All of us _____ computers at home.

    a. having

    b. has

    c. have

14. Does everyone _____ to class on time?

    a. come

    b. comes

    c. coming

15. Do many of the students _____ the computer lab?

    a. use

    b. using

    c. uses

16. Someone _____ a big car to school.

    a. drive

    b. driving

    c. drives

17. Most of the women are _____ dresses.

    a. wears

    b. wearing

    c. wear

18. A couple of us _____ doing our homework.

    a. is

    b. can

    c. are

19. Julie and Tom _____ very good students.

    a. is

    b. can

    c. are

20. Is _____ from Japan?

    a. all of us

    b. anyone

    c. none

Name _____ **Date** _____

Choose the best word or words to complete the sentence.

Example: Can _____ borrow your book?

   a. me

   ⓑ. I

   c. my

1. _____, you can.

   a. No

   b. Yes

   c. Not

2. _____ course.

   a. Of

   b. Ah

   c. Not

3. Could _____ go to the library?

   a. me

   b. my

   c. I

4. Wait until it opens, _____.

   a. please

   b. next

   c. thank you

5. I don't _____.

   a. understands

   b. understanding

   c. understand

6. Could _____ speak more slowly, please.

   a. you

   b. your

   c. his

7. Would you _____ this document for me? I don't read German.

   a. speak

   b. translate

   c. show

8. Would you _____ me your jacket? I'm cold.

   a. borrow

   b. borrows

   c. lend

9. Hello, may I _____ to Dr. Lopez, please?

   a. speak

   b. show

   c. help

10. Will you _____ me do my homework?

   a. speak

   b. show

   c. help

Read each sentence and choose the best way to word the request.

Example: You want to borrow your friend's pen.

    a. Can you borrow your pen, please?

    b. Can you borrow my pen, please?

    (c.) Could I borrow your pen, please?

11. You want to use your sister's computer.

    a. Can I lend your computer?

    b. Can I borrow my computer?

    c. Could I use your computer?

12. You want to see your friend's homework.

    a. Can I look at your homework?

    b. Could I look at my homework?

    c. Could you look at my homework?

13. You want to copy a page from your teacher's book.

    a. Could you copy a page from my book?

    b. Could I copy a page from your book?

    c. Could we copy a page from my book?

14. You want to use your friend's tape recorder.

    a. Could I use your tape recorder?

    b. Could I use my tape recorder?

    c. Could you use my tape recorder?

15. You don't understand something your teacher has just said.

    a. Can I explain you again?

    b. Can you explain it again?

    c. Can you borrow it again?

16. You are in the library and need to use the telephone.

    a. Could you use the phone?

    b. Could I lend the phone?

    c. Could I use the phone?

17. You want to bring your registration tomorrow.

    a. Can you bring my registration tomorrow?

    b. Can you bring your registration tomorrow?

    c. Can I bring my registration tomorrow?

18. You want your teacher to help you.

    a. Would I help you?

    b. Would you help you?

    c. Would you help me?

19. You need to speak to Mrs. Bongartz?

    a. Could I speak to Mrs. Bongartz?

    b. Would I speak to Mrs. Bongartz?

    c. Can me speak to Mrs. Bongartz?

20. You need an extra day to write your paper.

    a. Could you have an extra day to write my paper?

    b. Would I have an extra day to write your paper?

    c. Could I have an extra day to write my paper?

Book 2—Unit 8

Select the best word or words to complete each sentence.

Example: I'm _____ next year.

   a. going to graduate

   b. going to graduated

   c. go to graduate

1. She's _____ engineering.

   a. going to study

   b. going to studies

   c. go to study

2. _____ it going to be interesting?

   a. Is

   b. Are

   c. Can

3. _____ I going to China?

   a. Are

   b. Is

   c. Am

4. She _____ going to travel after the baby is born.

   a. can't

   b. aren't

   c. isn't

5. _____ you going to work in Texas after you graduate?

   a. Is

   b. Isn't

   c. Aren't

6. _____ they going to buy a new car?

   a. Are

   b. Is

   c. Isn't

7. Yes, you _____.

   a. is

   b. isn't

   c. are

8. No, you _____.

   a. is

   b. aren't

   c. are

9. Yes, we _____.

   a. is

   b. isn't

   c. are

10. No, she _____.

   a. is

   b. isn't

   c. aren't

11. _____ am I going to wait?

   a. How long

   b. What

   c. When does

12. When is Mary _____ her test?

   a. going to fly

   b. going to join

   c. going to take

13. When are Tom and Joan _____ married?

    a. going to start

    b. going to get

    c. going to take

14. When are you _____ your electric bill?

    a. going to pay

    b. going to visit

    c. going to finish

15. I'm _____ on Friday.

    a. going come

    b. going to come

    c. come

16. I'll take _____ home.

    a. him

    b. he

    c. his

17. Yes, he _____.

    a. going

    b. will

    c. won't

18. No, they _____.

    a. going

    b. will

    c. won't

19. _____ are they going to travel?

    a. Where

    b. What

    c. Who

20. _____ will be the new teacher?

    a. Where

    b. What

    c. Who

Book 2—Unit 9

Choose the words that describe each adjective.

Example: interesting
  a. one syllable
  b. two syllables ending with y
  c. two or more syllables not ending with y
  (c. is circled)

1. low
  a. one syllable
  b. two syllables ending with y
  c. two or more syllables not ending with y

2. noisy
  a. one syllable
  b. two syllables ending with y
  c. two or more syllables not ending with y

3. beautiful
  a. one syllable
  b. two syllables ending with y
  c. two or more syllables not ending with y

4. clean
  a. one syllable
  b. two syllables ending with y
  c. two or more syllables not ending with y

5. affordable
  a. one syllable
  b. two syllables ending with y
  c. two or more syllables not ending with y

6. quiet
  a. one syllable
  b. two syllables ending with y
  c. two or more syllables not ending with y

7. safe
  a. one syllable
  b. two syllables ending with y
  c. two or more syllables not ending with y

8. busy
  a. one syllable
  b. two syllables ending with y
  c. two or more syllables not ending with y

9. convenient
  a. one syllable
  b. two syllables ending with y
  c. two or more syllables not ending with y

10. dangerous
  a. one syllable
  b. two syllables ending with y
  c. two or more syllables not ending with y

Choose the comparative form of each adjective.

Example: clean
  a. cleaner than
  b. cleanier than
  c. cleanly
  (a. is circled)

11. good
  a. gooder than
  b. goodest than
  c. better

12. busy
    a. busy than
    b. busier than
    c. busher than

13. beautiful
    a. more beautiful than
    b. beautifuler than
    c. beautifulest than

14. far
    a. farrar than
    b. farther than
    c. farth than

15. warm
    a. warmly than
    b. warmest than
    c. warmer than

16. little
    a. less than
    b. more little than
    c. little than

17. populated
    a. populated than
    b. more populated than
    c. populatier than

18. bad
    a. badder than
    b. more bad than
    c. worse

19. safe
    a. saye than
    b. more safe than
    c. safer than

20. low
    a. lower than
    b. more low than
    c. lowlier than

Book 2—Unit 10

Select the best word or words to complete each sentence.

Example: A dog _____ read books.

  a. can
  b. can't

1. Dogs _____ eat food.
  a. can
  b. can't

2. Babies _____ drive cars.
  a. can
  b. can't

3. Cats _____ walk.
  a. can
  b. can't

4. Fish _____ swim.
  a. can
  b. can't

5. Bees _____ swim.
  a. can
  b. can't

6. I can _____ on the telephone.
  a. talk
  b. talks
  c. talking

7. She can _____ all night.
  a. studies
  b. studying
  c. study

8. They can _____ to Texas.
  a. drive
  b. drives
  c. driving

9. You can _____ a hamburger for lunch.
  a. eating
  b. eats
  c. eat

10. Tonight, we can _____ to the movies.
  a. go
  b. goes
  c. going

11. We can't _____ very well.
  a. dance
  b. dancing
  c. dances

12. They can't _____ to New York.
  a. flies
  b. fly
  c. flying

13. I can't _____ his name.
  a. remember
  b. remembering
  c. remembers

14. _____ you speak English? Yes, I can.
  a. Can
  b. Can't

15. Can you _____ Hungarian?

   a. ask

   b. speak

   c. apply

16. Can you _____ for a new job?

   a. take

   b. use

   c. apply

17. Can you _____ a hamburger in French?

   a. order

   b. practice

   c. read

18. Can you _____ the piano at night?

   a. read

   b. understand

   c. practice

19. Can you _____ Japanese with my friends?

   a. ask

   b. answer

   c. speak

20. Can you _____ a computer class next year?

   a. take

   b. fly

   c. ask

Name _____ Date _____

Select the best word or words to complete each sentence.

Example: I _____ to get home soon.

   a. has

   b. having

   ⓒ have

1. She _____ to eat breakfast.

   a. has

   b. having

   c. have

2. You _____ to work tomorrow.

   a. have

   b. has

   c. having

3. We _____ to go to class tonight.

   a. has

   b. having

   c. have

4. I _____ to eat three meals a day.

   a. have

   b. having

   c. has

5. My mother _____ to buy a new dress for the wedding.

   a. have

   b. has

   c. having

6. You _____ show your passport to the immigration officer.

   a. must to

   b. must

   c. musts

7. I _____ get some homework done tonight.

   a. musts

   b. must to

   c. must

8. She _____ visit her father on Sunday.

   a. musts

   b. must to

   c. must

9. We _____ get a marriage license.

   a. must to

   b. must

   c. musts

10. They _____ listen to the rabbi.

   a. must

   b. must to

   c. musts

11. You _____ to go to the wedding.

   a. don't has

   b. doesn't have

   c. don't have

12. They _____ to go on a honeymoon.

    a. don't has

    b. don't have

    c. doesn't have

13. She _____ to buy allergy medicine.

    a. don't has

    b. don't have

    c. doesn't have

14. I _____ to share the pizza with my wife.

    a. don't has

    b. don't have

    c. doesn't have

15. She _____ to wash the dishes every night.

    a. don't has

    b. don't have

    c. doesn't have

16. She _____ to be so sad.

    a. don't has

    b. don't have

    c. doesn't have

17. You _____ marry someone kind.

    a. should

    b. should be

    c. shoulds

18. I _____ work after I get married.

    a. shoulds

    b. should be

    c. should

19. They _____ have lots of children.

    a. shoulds

    b. should

    c. should be

20. He _____ a good father.

    a. shoulds

    b. should be

    c. should

Book 2—Unit 12

Choose the words that describes each adjective.

Example: beautiful

   a. one syllable

   b. two syllables ending with y

   (**c.**) two or more syllables not ending with y

1. fast

   a. one syllable

   b. two syllables ending with y

   c. two or more syllables not ending with y

2. busy

   a. one syllable

   b. two syllables ending with y

   c. two or more syllables not ending with y

3. effective

   a. one syllable

   b. two syllables ending with y

   c. two or more syllables not ending with y

4. sad

   a. one syllable

   b. two syllables ending with y

   c. two or more syllables not ending with y

5. ugly

   a. one syllable

   b. two syllables ending with y

   c. two or more syllables not ending with y

6. talkative

   a. one syllable

   b. two syllables ending with y

   c. two or more syllables not ending with y

7. dirty

   a. one syllable

   b. two syllables ending with y

   c. two or more syllables not ending with y

Find the superlative form of each word.

Example: powerful

   a. power

   (**b.**) most powerful

   c. powerfulest

8. dangerous

   a. dangerousless

   b. most dangerous

   c. dangeroust

9. good

   a. goodest

   b. betterest

   c. best

10. friendly

   a. most friendly

   b. more friendly

   c. friendliest

11. quiet

   a. most quiet

   b. quietest

   c. more quieter

12. talkative

   a. most talkative

   b. talkativest

   c. more talkativer

13. serious

   a. most serious

   b. more seriouser

   c. seriousest

14. bad

   a. baddest

   c. worstest

   c. worst

15. less

   a. lessest

   b. least

   c. more less

16. effective

   a. most effective

   b. effectivest

   c. more effectivest

17. affordable

   a. most affordable

   b. affordablest

   c. cheapest

18. more

   a. morest

   b. more more

   c. most

19. heavy

   a. most heavy

   b. heaviest

   c. heavierest

20. far

   a. fartherest

   b. most far

   c. farthest

Book 2—Unit 13

Name _____ **Date** _____

Select the best word or words to complete each sentence.

Example: Carter _____ a Democrat.

   a. were

   (b.) was

   c. weren't

1. Clara Barton and Susan B. Anthony _____ famous American women.

   a. were

   b. was

   c. weren't

2. _____ they Democrats?

   a. Were

   b. Was

   c. When

3. _____ he a Republican?

   a. What

   b. Was

   c. Were

4. Johnson _____ a Democrat.

   a. were

   b. was

   c. what

5. _____ he a president?

   a. What

   b. Was

   c. Were

6. Yes, you _____.

   a. was

   b. weren't

   c. were

7. Yes, he _____.

   a. wasn't

   b. were

   c. was

8. No, they _____.

   a. were

   b. weren't

   c. wasn't

9. Yes, we _____.

   a. were

   b. weren't

   c. wasn't

10. No, I _____.

   a. was

   b. wasn't

   c. were

11. No, you _____.

   a. were

   b. weren't

   c. wasn't

12. No, she _____.

   a. wasn't

   b. was

   c. weren't

13. _____ long was she in office?

   a. When

   b. Who

   c. How

14. _____ was president in 2000?

   a. When

   b. Who

   c. How

15. _____ was Lincoln president?

   a. When

   b. Who

   c. How

16. The _____ is the commander in chief.

   a. president

   b. vice president

   c. supreme court

17. The _____ was written in 1787.

   a. Congress

   b. Constitution

   c. population

18. _____ means to agree with.

   a. In favor

   b. Against

   c. Neutral

19. _____ means traditional.

   a. Liberal

   b. Democrat

   c. Conservative

20. _____ refers to laws.

   a. In favor

   b. Support

   c. Legislation

Book 2—Unit 14

Select the correct past tense word for each sentence.

Example: Last week, I _____ a new home.

    a. rent

    b. rant

    c. rented

1. Yesterday, John _____ his mother move into a smaller house.

    a. help

    b. helped

    c. helping

2. In the '70s, Tony and Mary _____ in Korea for three years.

    a. living

    b. lived

    c. live

3. The landlord _____ a broken door.

    a. faxed

    b. fix

    c. fixed

4. She _____ a cheap apartment.

    a. finded

    b. founded

    c. found

5. We _____ a lease.

    a. songed

    b. signed

    c. signing

6. They _____ their own apples.

    a. growed

    b. grown

    c. grew

7. We _____ for our house keys.

    a. looked

    b. looket

    c. looking

8. My parents _____ a beautiful table.

    a. buying

    b. buyed

    c. bought

9. My brother _____ a Subaru for five years.

    a. drive

    b. drove

    c. droved

10. Last year, Dad _____ my mother's favorite glass.

    a. broke

    b. brokt

    c. breaked

11. When _____ she move?

    a. don't

    b. do

    c. did

12. When _____ you paint the apartment?

    a. don't

    b. did

    c. do

13. _____ they like their old house?

   a. Didn't

   b. Does

   c. Doesn't

14. Last year, Joe and Nora _____ to move to Texas.

   a. want

   b. wanted

   c. wanting

15. We _____ on the street corner and waited for the bus.

   a. standed

   b. stand

   c. stood

16. Yes, it _____.

   a. do

   b. did

   c. didn't

17. No, they _____.

   a. doesn't

   b. did

   c. didn't

18. No, it _____.

   a. don't

   b. didn't

   c. did

19. Yes, I _____.

   a. did

   b. didn't

   c. does

20. No, we _____.

   a. doesn't

   b. didn't

   c. do

Name _____ **Date** _____

Choose the word or words that match the picture.

Example:

a. video
b. camera
c. compass

1.

a. compass
b. camera
c. scale

2.

a. nurse
b. first aid kit
c. sunblock

3.

a. fishing rod
b. flashlight
c. insect repellent

4.

a. cooler
b. fishing rod
c. flashlight

5.

a. tent
b. matches
c. sun block

Select the best word or words to complete each sentence.

Example: I plan _____ a fishing rod.

a. to bring
b. to write
c. to read

6. She plans _____ her new swimsuit.

a. wear
b. to wear
c. to dress

7. I hope _____ some birds in the sky.

a. have
b. see
c. to see

8. They plan _____ in the sun.

   a. keep

   b. to lie

   c. lie

9. Ann hopes _____ by the ocean.

   a. to camp

   b. sleep

   c. to catch

10. Bill wants _____ a big fish.

   a. take

   b. to catch

   c. to camp

11. _____ do I need to get a fishing license?

   a. Who

   b. When

   c. Plan

12. _____ you like to camp?

   a. Do

   b. When

   c. How

13. _____ are they going to get there?

   a. Do

   b. Is

   c. How

14. _____ you bring your flashlight?

   a. Does

   b. Did

   c. What

15. _____ she need to have sun block?

   a. Do

   b. What

   c. Does

16. They need _____ a ticket in advance.

   a. buy

   b. make

   c. to buy

17. I _____ to swim.

   a. take

   b. would

   c. like

18. She _____ study this afternoon.

   a. plans

   b. plans to

   c. plan to

19. It _____ be washed.

   a. have to

   b. has

   c. has to

20. They _____ go to the beach.

   a. hopes to

   b. hope to

   c. hope

Book 2—Unit 16

Choose the best word or words to complete each sentence.

Example: Joe _____ at 7:30 every morning.

   a. wake up

   b. get up

   (c.) wakes up

1. Tommy and Marilyn _____ for the party.

   a. have dressed

   b. has dressed

   c. gets dressed

2. When I hear the alarm clock, I _____ bed.

   a. jump

   b. jump on

   c. jump out of

3. She _____ her coat before she leaves the house.

   a. put off

   b. puts on

   c. put over

4. I _____ the children on my way to work.

   a. drop near

   b. drop far

   c. drop off

5. They _____ on Fridays.

   a. gets paid

   b. works hard

   c. get paid

6. He hates it when he's _____.

   a. stucks on traffic

   b. stuck on traffic

   c. stuck in traffic

7. When we get in the car, we _____ our seat belts.

   a. put off

   b. put on

   c. put in

8. Every morning, Ann _____ a shower.

   a. takes

   b. makes

   c. make

Indicate whether the underlined clause is the main clause or the time clause.

Example: They do their homework <u>after the children are in bed.</u>

   a. main clause

   (b.) time clause

9. In the evening, <u>the children practice the piano.</u>

   a. main clause

   b. time clause

10. <u>The teacher reads her book</u> while the students take the test.

   a. main clause

   b. time clause

11. What do you do <u>when school is over?</u>

    a. main clause

    b. time clause

12. <u>Do they do exercises</u> when they wake up?

    a. main clause

    b. time clause

13. <u>When I eat breakfast,</u> I don't eat lunch.

    a. main clause

    b. time clause

14. When I am going to have a test, <u>I study for a long time.</u>

    a. main clause

    b. time clause

Choose the best word or words to complete each sentence.

Example: _____ do you eat lunch?

    a. What

    (b.) When

    c. Do

15. _____ do you study?

    a. Where

    b. Are

    c. Is

16. _____ you eat at work?

    a. What

    b. When

    c. Do

17. _____ you going to fix dinner?

    a. Do

    b. Are

    c. When

18. _____ do you talk to when you need a raise?

    a. When

    b. Where

    c. Who

19. _____ I'm tired, I take a nap.

    a. When

    b. Who

    c. What

20. _____ did Millie lose her job?

    a. What

    b. Who

    c. When

Select the best word or words to complete the sentence.

Example: _____ your clothing.

   (a.) Put on

   b. Put off

   c. Put

1. The police officer _____ the tall fence.

   a. climbed in

   b. climbed over

   c. climbed into

2. The police put _____ the two robbers.

   a. handcuffs into

   b. handcuffs on

   c. handcuffs to

3. The robbers _____ a television and put it into the truck.

   a. picked up

   b. picked on

   c. picked by

4. The man _____ a window and broke his leg.

   a. looked out

   b. jumped up

   c. jumped out of

5. Tim stepped _____ a banana peel and slipped.

   a. on

   b. out of

   c. to

6. The criminals had to climb _____ the police car.

   a. under

   b. onto

   c. into

7. The dog _____ the old cat.

   a. climbed

   b. chased

   c. chase

8. They _____ in love twenty years ago.

   a. fall

   b. fell

   c. fells

9. _____ the fire truck arrived, half of the building had burned down.

   a. What

   b. That

   c. Before

10. She _____ the thieves.

   a. catched

   b. caught

   c. caughted

11. She started to run _____ the police arrived.

   a. as soon

   b. soon

   c. as soon as

12. _____ I went to sleep, the phone rang.

   a. As soon as

   b. Soon

   c. Soon as

13. They _____ a house after they got married.

   a. buyed

   b. bought

   c. boughted

14. _____ he went to the police station, he saw the thieves.

   a. Before

   b. What

   c. Why

15. Before I _____ a citizen, I studied a lot.

   a. becomed

   b. became

   c. becameth

16. After she _____ a baby, she stopped working.

   a. had

   b. having

   c. have

17. When he _____ his driver's license, he was very happy.

   a. get

   b. got

   c. getting

18. When she _____ to Mexico, she learned Spanish.

   a. came

   b. come

   c. coming

19. I was robbed _____ I got on the subway.

   a. after

   b. as soon

   c. what

20. _____ I leave my house, I always lock all the doors.

   a. Before

   b. After

   c. As soon

Book 2—Unit 18

Select the best word or words to complete the sentences.

Example: The dog _____ barking when the man came home.

   a. were

   (b.) was

   c. are

1. They _____ dancing when the music stopped.

   a. was

   b. were

   c. are

2. Officer Stone _____ eating dinner when his mother called.

   a. was

   b. were

   c. are

3. Lois _____ cooking.

   a. was

   b. were

   c. are

4. We _____ watching TV.

   a. is

   b. were

   c. was

5. You _____ taking a test.

   a. is

   b. was

   c. were

6. I _____ reading a book.

   a. were

   b. are

   c. was

7. They _____ listening to music.

   a. were

   b. is

   c. was

8. The officer _____ to find the thieves.

   a. try

   b. tried

   c. trying

9. Everyone _____ hungry.

   a. were

   b. was

   c. are

10. After she waited for two hours, she _____.

   a. leaving

   b. leaved

   c. left

11. They were sleeping _____ their daughter came home.

   a. what

   b. when

   c. why

12. I _____ a good movie.

 a. seen

 b. seeth

 c. saw

13. It _____ to rain after I got up.

 a. began

 b. begin

 c. beginned

14. The power _____ out.

 a. gone

 b. went

 c. goed

15. Mr. and Mrs. Jones _____ to the beach.

 a. driving

 b. drives

 c. drove

16. The child _____ home after school.

 a. walked

 b. walking

 c. walk

17. _____ I looked out the window, I heard a noise.

 a. What

 b. Why

 c. When

18. They _____ the fruit.

 a. cut

 b. cutted

 c. cuts

19. I _____ to work on time.

 a. gets

 b. got

 c. getting

20. My mother _____ dinner after my father gets home.

 a. cook

 b. cooked

 c. cooks

Book 3

Book 3 — Unit 1

Select the best word to complete each sentence.

Example: I _____ doing my homework.

   a. are

   b. is

   (c.) am

1. She _____ working today.

   a. isn't

   b. are

   c. not

2. The children _____ playing baseball.

   a. is

   b. are

   c. can

3. You _____ talking on the telephone.

   a. aren't

   b. isn't

   c. is

4. I _____ drinking.

   a. aren't

   b. isn't

   c. am not

5. We _____ sitting in the cafeteria.

   a. is

   b. are

   c. am

6. I _____ in Boston

   a. live

   b. lives

   c. living

7. You _____ biology.

   a. study

   b. studies

   c. studying

8. He _____ in a bank.

   a. work

   b. works

   c. working

9. We _____ three computers at home.

   a. has

   b. have

   c. having

10. The high school _____ students driving lessons.

   a. giving

   b. gives

   c. gives

11. I _____ eggs for breakfast.

   a. have

   b. has

   c. having

12. You _____ on Friday nights.

   a. dances

   b. has

   c. dance

13. I _____ study French.

   a. don't

   b. doesn't

   c. does

14. He _____ understand the book.

    a. don't

    b. do

    c. doesn't

15. Sally _____ go to school on Mondays.

    a. do

    b. don't

    c. doesn't

16. _____ is studying American history?

    a. Who

    b. Where

    c. When

17. Anne always _____ late.

    a. is come

    b. come

    c. is

18. _____ Inessa studying English?

    a. Is

    b. Are

    c. Can

19. Yes she _____.

    a. are

    b. is

    c. aren't

20. Where _____ they studying?

    a. is

    b. aren't

    c. are

Name _____ **Date** _____

Select the best word or words to complete each sentence.

Example: They _____ a movie.

  a. watches

  (b.) watch

  c. watching

1. _____, I walked to the restaurant.

  a. Tomorrow

  b. Now

  c. Yesterday

2. The children _____ very fast.

  a. grew

  b. grown

  c. grows

3. The Smiths _____ gone to bed.

  a. haves

  b. has

  c. have

4. Madeline _____ a new hat.

  a. buyed

  b. bought

  c. buy

5. Charles _____ wonderful books.

  a. writing

  b. written

  c. wrote

6. Eduardo _____ teach math.

  a. used to

  b. used

  c. use to

7. I used to _____ college students.

  a. advising

  b. advised

  c. advise

8. _____ the neighbors help you?

  a. Doing

  b. Did

  c. Does

9. The farmers _____ blue jeans.

  a. wore

  b. wearing

  c. weared

10. The mother _____ her new baby.

  a. holded

  b. hold

  c. held

11. _____ did the settlers live?

  a. Were

  b. Where

  c. What

12. _____ the trip long?

  a. Am

  b. Was

  c. Were

13. _____ the students ready for the test?

    a. Were

    b. Was

    c. Is

14. People _____ listen to them.

    a. does

    b. doesn't

    c. didn't

15. _____ the settlers live in Plymouth?

    a. Did

    b. Does

    c. Doesn't

16. In 1750, people _____ have TV.

    a. don't

    b. didn't

    c. do

17. Thomas _____ a big car.

    a. drive

    b. driving

    c. drove

18. Some colonists _____ French.

    a. spoke

    b. speaked

    c. spokes

19. It rained the day _____ yesterday.

    a. on

    b. after

    c. before

20. People didn't _____ to their pets.

    a. talkes

    b. talk

    c. talked

Book 3 — Unit 3

Select the best word or words to complete each sentence.

Example: I am _____ going to move.

   a. no

   (b.) not

   c. none

1. Jodi is _____ this weekend.

   a. going to leave

   b. going to leaves

   c. going to lefts

2. He _____ going to get married.

   a. are

   b. am

   c. is

3. They _____ going to stay.

   a. are no

   b. aren't

   c. are none

4. Sonny _____ going to move.

   a. are not

   b. is none

   c. isn't

5. Lisa and Marshall _____ a divorce.

   a. is going to have

   b. are get

   c. are going to get

6. _____ is she going to move to New York?

   a. When

   b. What

   c. Where

7. Lucy isn't going to live in Atlanta _____.

   a. any where

   b. any more

   c. any less

8. She is graduating _____.

   a. yesterday

   b. last night

   c. next month

9. When _____ they going to graduate?

   a. is

   b. are

   c. was

10. _____ is it going to rain?

   a. When

   b. What

   c. Can

11. Ann _____ to rent a new house.

   a. is going

   b. are going

   c. will

12. They _____ look for the keys.

   a. will

   b. are going

   c. is going

13. I _____ help my children.

   a. will

   b. am going

   c. going to

14. _____ will cook dinner?

   a. Who

   b. Where

   c. When

15. Before I graduate, I am going to _____ a job.

   a. finds

   b. found

   c. find

16. After she eats dinner, she's going _____ home.

   a. to go

   b. goes

   c. gone

17. _____ you going to take the train?

   a. Are

   b. Is

   c. When

18. Arthur _____ president of our company.

   a. was going

   b. is going to

   c. is going to be

19. Joanie is _____ take a vacation.

   a. going to still

   b. still going

   c. still going to

20. _____ a few minutes, I am going to eat a hamburger.

   a. On

   b. In

   c. And

Book 3 — Unit 4

Select the best description for each word.

Example: noisy
- a. one syllable
- **(b.)** two syllables ending in y
- c. two or more syllables not ending in y

1. modern
   - a. one syllable
   - b. two syllables ending in y
   - c. two or more syllables not ending in y

2. attractive
   - a. one syllable
   - b. two syllables ending in y
   - c. two or more syllables not ending in y

3. ugly
   - a. one syllable
   - b. two syllables ending in y
   - c. two or more syllables not ending in y

4. tall
   - a. one syllable
   - b. two syllables ending in y
   - c. two or more syllables not ending in y

5. convenient
   - a. one syllable
   - b. two syllables ending in y
   - c. two or more syllables not ending in y

Select the best word or words to complete each sentence.

Example: John's apartment was _____ than Mary's.
- a. more clean
- **(b.)** cleaner
- c. cleanest

6. That was the _____ hot dog in the world.
   - a. most bad
   - b. baddest
   - c. worst

7. She is the _____ student in the class.
   - a. brighter
   - b. brightest
   - c. brought

8. The new apartment is _____ than the old one.
   - a. most spacious
   - b. spaciouser
   - c. more spacious

9. She makes the _____ pie.
   - a. best
   - b. more good
   - c. more better

10. Mrs. Newman's class is the _____ one in the whole school.
    - a. most hard
    - b. hardest
    - c. harder

11. Which house is the _____?

    a. bigger

    b. big

    c. biggest

12. Which airport is the _____?

    a. convenienter

    b. most convenient

    c. conveniently

13. That neighborhood is the _____ in the city.

    a. more dangerous

    b. most dangerous

    c. dangerousest

14. She is _____ than her brother in math.

    a. better

    b. more good

    c. gooder

15. Maria's hair is _____ than Tanya's.

    a. shorter

    b. shortest

    c. more short

16. Which student is the _____?

    a. intelligentest

    b. intelligent

    c. most intelligent

17. Chicago is _____ away than New York.

    a. farthest

    b. farer

    c. farther

18. That is the _____ expensive one in the whole store.

    a. lesser

    b. least

    c. more less

19. He is the _____ man on television.

    a. more handsome

    b. most handsome

    c. handsomer

20. That is the _____ park in the city.

    a. most big

    b. biggerest

    c. biggest

Book 3 — Unit 5

Select the best word or words to complete each sentence.

Example: _____ it pretty?

   a. Are

   b. Am

   ©. Is

1. _____ she hungry?

   a. Are

   b. Am

   c. Is

2. _____ you late?

   a. Are

   b. Am

   c. Is

3. _____ they from Spain?

   a. Were

   b. Was

   c. Is

4. _____ he in Canada?

   a. Were

   b. Was

   c. Are

5. _____ it raining?

   a. Were

   b. Is

   c. Are

6. _____ they eat pizza?

   a. Does

   b. Doesn't

   c. Do

7. _____ he study Japanese?

   a. Do

   b. Don't

   c. Does

8. _____ you like French movies?

   a. Do

   b. Does

   c. Doesn't

9. _____ has a cellular telephone?

   a. Whom

   b. Whose

   c. Who

10. _____ coat is red?

   a. Whose

   b. Who's

   c. Who

11. _____ is going home early?

   a. Whose

   b. Who's

   c. Who

12. How _____ is it to Paris?

   a. longer

   b. far

   c. shorter

13. How _____ children do you have?

   a. much

   b. long

   c. many

14. How _____ money does she make?

   a. much

   b. long

   c. many

15. Yes, I _____.

   a. didn't

   b. do

   c. don't

16. No, I _____.

   a. don't

   b. does

   c. doesn't

17. Yes, he _____.

   a. won't

   b. will

   c. do

18. No, we _____.

   a. doesn't

   b. do

   c. didn't

19. No, she _____.

   a. weren't

   b. wasn't

   c. aren't

20. She is from China, _____?

   a. isn't she

   b. not she

   c. is she

Book 3 — Unit 6

Name _____ Date _____

Select the best word or words to complete each sentence.

Example: I don't know what Lucy is doing. She _____ be listening to the baseball game.

   a. must

   (b.) might

   c. maybe

1. The child _____ a doctor's appointment.

   a. might need

   b. might be

   c. must be

2. Yes, _____ go to Germany.

   a. Hans won't be

   b. Hans might

   c. may not

3. No, _____ eat at the Italian restaurant.

   a. they won't

   b. they might be

   c. might

4. Cindy _____ take a class this summer.

   a. mights

   b. might be

   c. might

5. John _____ to Japan.

   a. may travels

   b. maybe travel

   c. may travel

6. It _____ tomorrow.

   a. may rain

   b. may rains

   c. maybe rain

7. Timothy _____ when the doctor explains it.

   a. will be understand

   b. will understands

   c. will understand

8. David _____ a stomach ache.

   a. might have

   b. will

   c. must

9. Sylvia _____ today.

   a. might

   b. might no visit

   c. might not visit

10. Sam _____ at the dentist's office.

   a. might

   b. may is

   c. must be

11. He _____ at the store.

   a. could

   b. could be

   c. couldn't

12. They _____ happier.

   a. couldn't

   b. couldn't be

   c. could

13. You _____ English.

   a. must like

   b. must likes

   c. musts like

14. He _____ a new program.

   a. might see

   b. mights sees

   c. mights see

15. Mary _____ be a nurse.

   a. could yes

   b. could not

   c. could no

16. After this class, he _____ studying English.

   a. might continue

   b. may continues

   c. maybe continue

17. I _____ to play the piano.

   a. could learns

   b. could learn

   c. could learning

18. They _____ working at the store.

   a. might are

   b. may are

   c. might be

19. It _____ easier.

   a. could

   b. could be

   c. couldn't

20. Tony _____ like hamburgers.

   a. must not

   b. must no

   c. might no

Book 3 — Unit 7

Name _____ Date _____

Choose the best word or words to complete each sentence.

Example: I _____ pay taxes.

   (a.) must

   b. must no

   c. musts

1. I _____ work

   a. have

   b. have to

   c. has

2. Mrs. Taylor _____ stop at a red light.

   a. have to

   b. has

   c. has to

3. A driver _____ drive over the speed limit.

   a. must no

   b. must not

   c. must to

4. Children _____ to wear uniforms to school.

   a. didn't has

   b. don't has

   c. don't have

5. Michael _____ to work on Sundays.

   a. doesn't have

   b. doesn't has

   c. don't has

6. I _____ to study for my exam.

   a. doesn't have

   b. don't have

   c. don't has

7. The Wilsons _____ the party.

   a. not go

   b. cannot go to

   c. cannot go

8. Tommy _____ work today.

   a. cannot go to

   b. cannot goes to

   c. cannot go

9. It _____ 50 miles an hour.

   a. can go

   b. can goes

   c. can going

10. He _____ drive a truck without a license.

   a. can no

   b. cannot

   c. can to

11. Marie _____ French.

   a. can speak

   b. can speaks

   c. can speaking

12. Susie and Ronnie _____ the test on Friday.

   a. can taking

   b. can takes

   c. can take

13. I _____ for the test.

   a. should study

   b. should studies

   c. should studying

14. They _____ not drink and drive.

   a. should

   b. shoulds

   c. should no

15. It _____ cost so much to get a license.

   a. should no

   b. shouldn't

   c. shoulds not

16. She _____ more slowly.

   a. should drive

   b. should drives

   c. should driving

17. They _____ go to Spain this month.

   a. shouldn't

   b. should no

   c. shoulds

18. You _____ get a driver's license.

   a. have better

   b. had better

   c. has better

19. She _____ go to Iceland.

   a. have better

   b. has better

   c. had better

20. They _____ up.

   a. have better hurry

   b. had better hurries

   c. had better hurry

Book 3 — Unit 8

Choose the best word or words to complete each sentence.

Example: Tom and Rita _____ watched 200 videos.

   a. has

   (b.) have

   c. having

1. It _____ all morning long.

   a. has rained

   b. have raining

   c. had raining

2. She _____ all of the mail.

   a. has opening

   b. has opened

   c. have opened

3. We have lived in Boston _____ 1985.

   a. since

   b. for

   c. of

4. We walked _____ two hours.

   a. since

   b. for

   c. of

5. She has studied English _____ five years.

   a. for

   b. since

   c. of

6. I have been married _____ month.

   a. since

   b. of

   c. for

7. They have lived here _____ March.

   a. since

   b. of

   c. for

8. Lois has worked in a hospital _____ 1985.

   a. since

   b. of

   c. for

9. We _____ listened to classical music in the park.

   a. have

   b. has

   c. hasn't

10. I have _____ planned the wedding.

   a. yet

   b. already

   c. since

11. I haven't done my homework _____.

   a. since

   b. already

   c. yet

12. They have studied _____ they came home.

   a. since

   b. already

   c. yet

13. _____ you watched the videos?

   a. Has

   b. Have

   c. Having

14. _____ she gotten divorced?

   a. Has

   b. Have

   c. Having

15. _____, I haven't.

   a. Not

   b. No

   c. Yes

16. _____, they have.

   a. Yes

   b. Not

   c. No

17. No, it _____.

   a. have no

   b. haven't

   c. hasn't

18. _____ have you worked in New York?

   a. How many

   b. How

   c. How long

19. _____ times have you been to London?

   a. How many

   b. How

   c. How long

20. She has _____ her own restaurant.

   a. open

   b. opening

   c. opened

Name _____ **Date** _____

Select the best word or words to complete each sentence.

Example: We _____ received 20 applications.

   a. having

   b. has

   (c.) have

1. She _____ a break for lunch.

   a. has taken

   b. has takes

   c. has took

2. He has _____ two envelopes.

   a. made for

   b. addressed

   c. filled by

3. Tony has _____ gone home early.

   a. so

   b. all

   c. always

4. It is only 8:00 A.M. and she has received five faxes _____.

   a. just

   b. so far

   c. never

5. They _____ work late.

   a. so far

   b. often

   c. never to

6. You need to _____ a form.

   a. fill of

   b. fill back

   c. fill out

7. Mrs. Johnson _____ on time.

   a. always arrived

   b. arrival always

   c. always arriven

8. They had _____ mistakes.

   a. made often

   b. often made

   c. to made often

9. She has cooked _____.

   a. from time to time

   b. back time to time

   c. behind times to times

10. Dr. Bach _____.

   a. has late stayed a few times

   b. has stayed a few times

   c. has stayed late a few times

11. The children _____ a problem.

   a. rarely had

   b. rarely to

   c. rarely has

12. When I am ill, I _____ sick.

    a. call over

    b. call back

    c. call in

13. _____ you ever eaten tacos?

    a. Has to

    b. Has

    c. Have

14. _____ company do you work for?

    a. How

    b. What

    c. Where

15. Yes, she _____.

    a. has

    b. haven't

    c. haves

16. _____ he ever had a job interview?

    a. Has

    b. Have

    c. Haven't

17. No, they _____.

    a. hasn't

    b. has

    c. haven't

18. _____ you ever worked in a hospital?

    a. Has

    b. Have

    c. Hasn't

19. Yes, it _____.

    a. has

    b. haven't

    c. hasn't

20. _____ Tony and Mary traded to Germany?

    a. Have

    b. Has

    c. Have no

Book 3 — Unit 10

Select the best word or words to complete each sentence.

Example: The game started _____ hour ago.

   a. of

   b. by

   ⓒ an

1. I have been watching the game _____.

   a. for an hour

   b. since an hour

   c. of an hour

2. Jason has been playing piano _____.

   a. for 1989

   b. since 1989

   c. of 1989

3. Ms. Km has been flying _____ nine hours.

   a. of

   b. since

   c. for

4. She has been catching _____.

   a. for balls

   b. slow balls

   c. at balls

5. I have been drinking coffee _____ I arrived at work.

   a. since

   b. for

   c. from

6. Mr. Amarsh has been waiting _____ an hour.

   a. of

   b. for

   c. since

7. You _____ been watching the game.

   a. hasn't

   b. has

   c. have

8. It _____ been sunny.

   a. has

   b. have

   c. haven't

9. We have been living in New York _____ 10 years.

   a. of

   b. since

   c. for

10. _____ is the dog doing?

   a. Who

   b. How

   c. When

11. We _____ been watching the game.

   a. have no

   b. has

   c. haven't

12. Yes, it _____.

    a. are

    b. is

    c. aren't

13. How _____ has she been teaching Chinese?

    a. many

    b. many of

    c. long

14. How _____ books has he sold?

    a. long

    b. many

    c. many of

15. No, he _____.

    a. aren't

    b. isn't

    c. is

16. No, they _____.

    a. aren't

    b. isn't

    c. is

17. Yes, we _____.

    a. aren't

    b. isn't

    c. are

18. No, he _____.

    a. doesn't

    b. do

    c. don't

19. No, they _____.

    a. doesn't

    b. do

    c. don't

20. No, they _____.

    a. have

    b. haven't

    c. are

Book 3 — Unit 11

Select the best word or words to complete each sentence.

Example: She _____ ice cream.

   a. loving

   b. love

   (**c.**) loves

1. They _____ graduate in June.

   a. hopes to

   b. hope

   c. hope to

2. Marsha _____ married when she is 25.

   a. plans get

   b. plans to get

   c. plan to get

3. He _____ to drive a truck.

   a. know how

   b. knowing how

   c. knows how

4. My mother has offered _____ for my son's education.

   a. pay

   b. to pay

   c. paying

5. Mrs. Jones intends _____ on time

   a. arrives

   b. to arrive

   c. arrive

6. I would like _____ at the local hospital.

   a. to volunteer

   b. volunteer

   c. to volunteering

7. My teacher _____ to finish college.

   a. me persuaded

   b. persuaded me

   c. persuading

8. The airlines are going _____ a ticket.

   a. me to send

   b. to me

   c. to send me

9. His doctor _____ more vegetables.

   a. asked him

   b. asked him to

   c. asked him to eat

10. They _____ in school.

   a. hope to start their children

   b. hope start

   c. hope start children their

11. I _____ back to school.

   a. him asked to

   b. asked him to go

   c. asked go

12. They _____ us about the fire.

    a. needed to tell

    b. need to told

    c. need told

13. Mrs. Jones _____ a secretary.

    a. hired

    b. forbidding

    c. convince

14. It's _____ learn to use the computer.

    a. smart

    b. smart to

    c. enable to

15. It's _____ earn money.

    a. hard

    b. easy

    c. hard to

16. It's _____ cook.

    a. difficult not

    b. difficult

    c. not difficult to

17. It's _____ search for happiness.

    a. easy to

    b. easy

    c. too easy

18. _____ good food is a joy.

    a. Eat

    b. To

    c. To eat

19. _____ hard is good for the soul.

    a. Work

    b. Too

    c. To work

20. _____ a dog is a responsibility.

    a. Own

    b. To own

    c. Own too

Book 3 — Unit 12

Select the best word or words to complete each sentence.

Example: She _____ her children with babysitters.

  a. hated to leaving

  b. hated leaving

  c. hating left

1. They _____ to Greece.

  a. anticipates to going

  b. anticipate to go

  c. anticipated going

2. Maggie _____ the dentist.

  a. postponing

  b. postponed seeing

  c. postpone see

3. I _____ for my little brother.

  a. resented working

  b. resents working

  c. resented work

4. Yesterday, the children _____ their test at 1:00.

  a. starts taking

  b. started taking

  c. starting taking

5. John thought _____ going to medical school.

  a. about

  b. for

  c. to

6. They are hoping _____ pass the exam.

  a. to

  b. from

  c. of

7. He is planning _____ moving to a house.

  a. from

  b. on

  c. of

8. We are proud _____ our children.

  a. from

  b. on

  c. of

9. I am worried _____ paying my bills.

  a. of

  b. about

  c. from

10. I am fond _____ ice cream.

  a. of

  b. from

  c. by

11. She is afraid _____ snakes.

  a. of

  b. from

  c. to

12. You can count _____ me to help you.

  a. from

  b. of

  c. on

13. Don't worry _____ me.

    a. from

    b. about

    c. on

14. Please dream _____ happy things.

    a. on

    b. from

    c. about

15. Don't blame him _____ your troubles.

    a. for

    b. of

    c. from

16. I am looking forward _____ my vacation.

    a. to

    b. of

    c. for

17. My wife and I argue _____ money.

    a. from

    b. of

    c. about

18. He's good _____ sports.

    a. at

    b. by

    c. from

19. She's guilty _____ murder.

    a. of

    b. behind

    c. from

20. I lived here _____ 10 years.

    a. of

    b. for

    c. behind

Book 3 — Unit 13

Find the best word or words to complete each sentence.

Example: Dresses are _____ in New York.

   (**a.**) designed

   b. designer

   c. designate

1. Salmon is _____ in Alaska.

   a. catched

   b. caught

   c. claught

2. Strawberries are _____ in Watsonville, California.

   a. growth

   b. growed

   c. grown

3. Corn is _____ in Iowa.

   a. raised

   b. raisin

   c. raiseth

4. Grapes are _____ in California.

   a. pickered

   b. picked

   c. picken

5. In Florida, oranges are _____ by a machine.

   a. squeezed

   b. squeezein

   c. squeeze

6. The clothes are _____ in the Laundromat.

   a. washing

   b. washed

   c. washes

7. The apples _____ by truck.

   a. transported

   b. are transported

   c. transporting

8. The workers _____ the carrots.

   a. cut

   b. are cut

   c. cutted

9. Silver _____ in Mexico.

   a. miner

   b. is mined

   c. mined

10. The artists _____ beautiful paintings.

   a. produces

   b. produced

   c. are produced

11. Where are razors _____?

   a. maked

   b. are made

   c. made

12. Refrigerators are manufactured _____ General Electric.

   a. of

   b. to

   c. by

13. Children _____ English.

   a. are study

   b. study

   c. studies

14. Where are carrots _____?

   a. growed

   b. grow

   c. grown

15. After the oranges _____, they are taken by truck to the cannery.

   a. pick

   b. are picked

   c. picked

16. What kind of cake _____ with ice cream?

   a. is served

   b. served

   c. serve

17. The workers _____ the cheese in the refrigerator.

   a. stored

   b. is stored

   c. storing

18. _____ tobacco grown in North Carolina?

   a. Is

   b. Did

   c. Why

19. _____ tomatoes grown?

   a. Where

   b. Where are

   c. Are where

20. Chickens _____ in Michigan.

   a. are raised

   b. raised

   c. is raised

Book 3 — Unit 14

Select the best word or words to complete each sentence.

Example: The child _____ the camera.

    a. is held

    b. holden

    (c.) held

1. The meal _____ by the family.

    a. eaten

    b. was eaten

    c. eats

2. The dentist _____ the tooth.

    a. was pulled

    b. pulled

    c. pulling

3. The newspaper _____ .

    a. torn

    b. was torn

    c. tearing

4. Laser surgery _____ by an eye doctor.

    a. performed

    b. was performing

    c. was performed

5. The structure _____ in 1921.

    a. built

    b. was building

    c. was built

6. A good lunch _____ by the cook.

    a. was prepared

    b. prepared

    c. was preparing

7. The tour guide _____ for three hours.

    a. talked

    b. was talked

    c. talking

8. The patient _____ a heart transplant.

    a. was wanted

    b. wanted

    c. wanting

9. The major problem _____ the cost.

    a. were

    b. are

    c. is

10. A cup of coffee _____ for the customer.

    a. was preparing

    b. prepared

    c. was prepared

11. The car _____ of steel.

    a. made

    b. is making

    c. is made

12. The slaves _____ simple tools.

    a. used

    b. was used

    c. is used

13. The repairs _____ in a week.

    a. will completed

    b. will be completion

    c. will be completed

14. The windows _____.

    a. are being washed

    b. being washed

    c. were washing

15. The book _____ in August.

    a. was written

    b. may written

    c. be written

16. The report _____ by the committee.

    a. was approving

    b. was approved

    c. was approve

17. Where is the Eiffel Tower _____?

    a. location of

    b. was approved

    c. located

18. Where were the papers _____?

    a. filing

    b. filed

    c. filing

19. When was it _____?

    a. produced

    b. produce

    c. producing

20. When _____ the pie be baked?

    a. were

    b. was

    c. will

Name _____ **Date** _____

Select the best word or words to complete each sentence.

Example: _____ you going to buy boots?

   a. Is

   b. Was

   © Are

1. _____ many CDs do you want?

   a. Where

   b. Who

   c. How

2. The car, _____ is yellow, is on the street.

   a. which

   b. who

   c. where

3. Tony, _____ cats cry all the time, is never home.

   a. who

   b. whose

   c. which

4. The woman _____ cooks Italian food loves it.

   a. whose

   b. who's

   c. who

5. The jeep came from Alaska, _____ it was used in the wilderness.

   a. where

   b. when

   c. who

6. The actor, _____ the audience adored, was extremely talented.

   a. whose

   b. whom

   c. who

7. _____ singer do you like?

   a. Who

   b. Which

   c. When

8. The musician, _____ refuses to fly, rented a car.

   a. who

   b. whom

   c. which

9. _____ coat is this?

   a. Whom

   b. Whose

   c. Where

10. _____ did you go?

   a. What

   b. Who

   c. Where

11. _____ has such pretty black hair?

   a. When

   b. Who

   c. Where

12. Books, _____ are printed in my language, are hard to find.

   a. who

   b. where

   c. which

13. New York City, _____ is located in New York State, is my favorite city.

   a. who

   b. where

   c. which

14. The Blues Diner, _____ features soul food, is my favorite restaurant.

   a. which

   b. who

   c. where

15. _____ many musicians did you see?

   a. Who

   b. How

   c. Where

16. Cher, _____ is a famous singer, gave a concert there.

   a. whom

   b. whose

   c. who

17. Tony, _____ house we are in right now, is out of town this week.

   a. whose

   b. where

   c. who

18. Haggis comes from Scotland, _____ it is considered a delicacy.

   a. when

   b. where

   c. who

19. _____ one did you like best?

   a. Where

   b. Who

   c. Which

20. Did you ask _____ many people had arrived?

   a. how

   b. which

   c. what

Answer Key

Basic—Answer Key

Unit 1

1. c
2. b
3. a
4. a
5. b
6. c
7. a
8. c
9. c
10. b
11. c
12. c
13. b
14. a
15. b
16. c
17. a
18. c
19. c
20. a

Unit 2

1. a
2. c
3. b
4. c
5. a
6. a
7. c
8. c
9. a
10. a
11. c
12. b
13. b
14. a
15. c
16. b
17. a
18. a
19. b
20. b

Unit 3

1. c
2. b
3. a
4. b
5. a
6. c
7. b
8. c
9. c
10. a
11. c
12. b
13. c
14. c
15. a
16. a
17. c
18. a
19. a
20. a

Unit 4

1. a
2. b
3. c
4. b
5. a
6. c
7. c
8. a
9. c
10. b
11. c
12. b
13. a
14. c
15. b
16. a
17. b
18. c
19. a
20. a

Unit 5

1. c
2. b
3. c
4. a
5. c
6. a
7. a
8. c
9. a
10. a
11. c
12. c
13. a
14. b
15. c
16. b
17. a
18. c
19. b
20. a

Unit 6

1. c
2. b
3. c
4. a
5. b
6. a
7. a
8. c
9. c
10. a
11. b
12. a
13. a
14. c
15. a
16. a
17. c
18. a
19. a
20. b

Unit 7

1. c
2. a
3. a
4. a
5. c
6. b
7. c
8. a
9. c
10. a
11. b
12. c
13. a
14. c
15. a
16. c
17. a
18. b
19. c
20. b

Unit 8

1. a
2. a
3. b
4. c
5. c
6. b
7. a
8. b
9. c
10. a
11. b
12. c
13. a
14. b
15. a
16. b
17. c
18. c
19. b
20. b

Unit 9

1. b
2. c
3. b
4. a
5. a
6. b
7. c
8. b
9. c
10. b
11. a
12. a
13. b
14. c
15. a
16. c
17. c
18. c
19. b
20. c

Unit 10

1. b
2. c
3. c
4. a
5. c
6. b
7. c
8. c
9. b
10. b
11. c
12. c
13. c
14. a
15. b
16. c
17. b
18. b
19. b
20. a

Unit 11

1. b
2. c
3. a
4. b
5. a
6. b
7. c
8. c
9. a
10. b
11. a
12. a
13. a
14. c
15. b
16. c
17. a
18. c
19. c
20. b

Unit 12

1. b
2. c
3. a
4. b
5. c
6. a
7. c
8. c
9. a
10. c
11. b
12. a
13. c
14. c
15. b
16. c
17. a
18. c
19. b
20. b

Unit 13

1. b
2. a
3. a
4. c
5. a
6. c
7. b
8. a
9. b
10. c
11. b
12. c
13. b
14. b
15. b
16. c
17. a
18. b
19. c
20. a

Unit 14

1. c
2. b
3. c
4. b
5. a
6. a
7. c
8. c
9. a
10. c
11. b
12. b
13. b
14. c
15. a
16. c
17. a
18. b
19. b
20. c

Unit 15

1. c
2. a
3. b
4. a
5. a
6. a
7. b
8. c
9. c
10. c
11. c
12. c
13. c
14. c
15. c
16. a
17. b
18. a
19. a
20. a

Book 1—Answer Key

Unit 1

1. b
2. b
3. c
4. a
5. b
6. a
7. b
8. a
9. c
10. b
11. a
12. c
13. c
14. a
15. b
16. a
17. b
18. c
19. a
20. a

Unit 2

1. a
2. b
3. c
4. a
5. a
6. b
7. c
8. a
9. b
10. c
11. b
12. a
13. c
14. c
15. a
16. b
17. a
18. a
19. a
20. b

Unit 3

1. a
2. b
3. b
4. b
5. a
6. b
7. b
8. b
9. b
10. a
11. c
12. a
13. b
14. c
15. a
16. b
17. c
18. b
19. a
20. b

Unit 4

1. a
2. c
3. b
4. c
5. c
6. b
7. b
8. c
9. c
10. b
11. a
12. b
13. a
14. b
15. c
16. a
17. a
18. b
19. a
20. b

Unit 5

1. c
2. b
3. c
4. a
5. b
6. a
7. a
8. b
9. a
10. c
11. a
12. c
13. a
14. c
15. b
16. a
17. a
18. c
19. c
20. c

Unit 6

1. b
2. a
3. b
4. a
5. a
6. c
7. c
8. b
9. c
10. c
11. c
12. a
13. b
14. a
15. b
16. a
17. c
18. c
19. b
20. c

Unit 7

1. b
2. a
3. b
4. b
5. a
6. c
7. b
8. a
9. a
10. c
11. a
12. b
13. c
14. a
15. c
16. b
17. c
18. c
19. b
20. a

Unit 8

1. a
2. b
3. c
4. b
5. c
6. c
7. b
8. c
9. b
10. b
11. c
12. b
13. a
14. a
15. a
16. c
17. c
18. a
19. a
20. b

Unit 9

1. c
2. b
3. c
4. c
5. a
6. c
7. b
8. c
9. c
10. b
11. c
12. a
13. c
14. a
15. a
16. c
17. c
18. a
19. c
20. b

Unit 10

1. c
2. b
3. c
4. b
5. a
6. b
7. a
8. c
9. c
10. c
11. b
12. a
13. b
14. a
15. c
16. a
17. b
18. a
19. b
20. a

Unit 11

1. b
2. b
3. c
4. a
5. b
6. c
7. c
8. a
9. b
10. c
11. a
12. c
13. a
14. a
15. b
16. a
17. a
18. c
19. c
20. a

Unit 12

1. b
2. b
3. c
4. a
5. c
6. a
7. c
8. a
9. c
10. b
11. c
12. b
13. a
14. b
15. c
16. a
17. c
18. c
19. b
20. a

Unit 13

1. a
2. a
3. b
4. b
5. a
6. c
7. c
8. b
9. c
10. c
11. b
12. a
13. a
14. b
15. c
16. b
17. a
18. a
19. a
20. c

Unit 14

1. a
2. a
3. a
4. b
5. a
6. c
7. b
8. a
9. b
10. b
11. b
12. b
13. a
14. c
15. c
16. a
17. a
18. a
19. c
20. c

Unit 15

1. a
2. b
3. c
4. b
5. b
6. a
7. b
8. b
9. a
10. c
11. c
12. b
13. c
14. a
15. a
16. c
17. a
18. c
19. c
20. b

Unit 16

1. b
2. b
3. c
4. a
5. a
6. b
7. c
8. a
9. b
10. c
11. b
12. a
13. a
14. b
15. a
16. a
17. c
18. c
19. a
20. b

Unit 17

1. b
2. a
3. a
4. a
5. b
6. b
7. a
8. c
9. a
10. b
11. a
12. a
13. c
14. b
15. a
16. b
17. a
18. c
19. b
20. b

Unit 18

1. a
2. c
3. a
4. c
5. a
6. c
7. b
8. c
9. c
10. a
11. a
12. a
13. b
14. c
15. b
16. a
17. a
18. a
19. c
20. b

Book 2— Answer Key

Unit 1

1. a
2. b
3. b
4. a
5. b
6. b
7. c
8. b
9. c
10. a
11. c
12. b
13. b
14. c
15. c
16. b
17. a
18. c
19. b
20. b

Unit 2

1. b
2. b
3. c
4. b
5. c
6. a
7. b
8. a
9. a
10. c
11. c
12. b
13. c
14. c
15. a
16. c
17. a
18. b
19. a
20. b

Unit 3

1. b
2. a
3. a
4. b
5. b
6. c
7. a
8. c
9. a
10. b
11. a
12. a
13. b
14. b
15. a
16. a
17. c
18. a
19. c
20. a

Unit 4

1. a
2. b
3. a
4. b
5. c
6. b
7. a
8. b
9. a
10. a
11. b
12. b
13. a
14. b
15. a
16. a
17. b
18. c
19. c
20. a

Unit 5

1. b
2. c
3. b
4. b
5. a
6. b
7. b
8. a
9. a
10. b
11. a
12. c
13. a
14. c
15. a
16. b
17. c
18. b
19. c
20. c

Unit 6

1. b
2. a
3. c
4. a
5. b
6. c
7. c
8. c
9. a
10. a
11. c
12. b
13. c
14. a
15. a
16. c
17. b
18. c
19. c
20. b

Unit 7

1. b
2. a
3. c
4. a
5. c
6. a
7. b
8. c
9. a
10. c
11. c
12. a
13. b
14. a
15. b
16. c
17. c
18. c
19. a
20. c

Unit 8

1. a
2. a
3. c
4. c
5. c
6. a
7. c
8. b
9. c
10. b
11. a
12. c
13. b
14. a
15. b
16. a
17. b
18. c
19. a
20. c

Unit 9

1. a
2. b
3. c
4. a
5. c
6. c
7. a
8. b
9. c
10. c
11. c
12. b
13. a
14. b
15. c
16. a
17. b
18. c
19. c
20. a

Unit 10

1. a
2. b
3. a
4. a
5. b
6. a
7. c
8. a
9. c
10. a
11. a
12. b
13. a
14. a
15. b
16. c
17. a
18. c
19. c
20. a

Unit 11

1. a
2. a
3. c
4. a
5. a
6. a
7. a
8. a
9. a
10. a
11. c
12. b
13. c
14. b
15. c
16. c
17. c
18. c
19. c
20. b

Unit 12

1. a
2. b
3. c
4. a
5. b
6. c
7. b
8. b
9. c
10. c
11. b
12. a
13. a
14. c
15. b
16. a
17. a
18. c
19. b
20. c

Unit 13

1. a
2. a
3. b
4. b
5. b
6. c
7. c
8. b
9. a
10. c
11. b
12. a
13. c
14. b
15. a
16. a
17. b
18. a
19. c
20. c

Unit 14

1. b
2. b
3. c
4. c
5. b
6. c
7. a
8. c
9. b
10. a
11. c
12. b
13. a
14. b
15. c
16. b
17. c
18. b
19. a
20. b

Unit 15

1. a
2. b
3. a
4. c
5. b
6. b
7. c
8. b
9. a
10. b
11. b
12. a
13. c
14. b
15. c
16. c
17. c
18. b
19. c
20. b

Unit 16

1. a
2. c
3. b
4. c
5. c
6. c
7. b
8. a
9. a
10. a
11. b
12. a
13. b
14. a
15. a
16. c
17. b
18. c
19. a
20. c

Unit 17

1. b
2. b
3. a
4. c
5. a
6. c
7. b
8. b
9. c
10. b
11. c
12. a
13. b
14. a
15. b
16. a
17. b
18. a
19. a
20. a

Unit 18

1. b
2. a
3. a
4. b
5. c
6. c
7. a
8. b
9. b
10. c
11. b
12. c
13. a
14. b
15. c
16. a
17. c
18. a
19. b
20. c

Book 3 — Answer Key

Unit 1

1. a
2. b
3. a
4. c
5. b
6. a
7. a
8. b
9. b
10. b
11. a
12. c
13. a
14. c
15. c
16. a
17. c
18. a
19. b
20. c

Unit 2

1. c
2. a
3. c
4. b
5. c
6. a
7. c
8. b
9. a
10. c
11. b
12. b
13. a
14. c
15. a
16. b
17. c
18. a
19. c
20. b

Unit 3

1. a
2. c
3. b
4. c
5. c
6. a
7. b
8. c
9. b
10. a
11. a
12. a
13. a
14. a
15. c
16. a
17. a
18. c
19. c
20. b

Unit 4

1. c
2. c
3. b
4. a
5. c
6. c
7. b
8. c
9. a
10. b
11. c
12. b
13. b
14. a
15. a
16. c
17. c
18. b
19. b
20. c

Unit 5

1. c
2. a
3. a
4. b
5. b
6. c
7. c
8. a
9. c
10. a
11. c
12. b
13. c
14. a
15. b
16. a
17. b
18. c
19. b
20. a

Unit 6

1. a
2. b
3. a
4. c
5. c
6. a
7. c
8. a
9. c
10. c
11. b
12. b
13. a
14. a
15. b
16. a
17. b
18. c
19. b
20. a

Unit 7

1. b
2. c
3. b
4. c
5. .a
6. b
7. b
8. a
9. a
10. b
11. a
12. c
13. a
14. a
15. b
16. a
17. a
18. b
19. c
20. c

Unit 8

1. a
2. b
3. a
4. b
5. a
6. c
7. a
8. a
9. a
10. b
11. c
12. a
13. b
14. a
15. b
16. a
17. c
18. c
19. a
20. c

Unit 9

1. a
2. b
3. c
4. b
5. b
6. c
7. a
8. b
9. a
10. c
11. a
12. c
13. c
14. b
15. a
16. a
17. c
18. b
19. a
20. a

151

Unit 10

1. a
2. b
3. c
4. b
5. a
6. b
7. c
8. a
9. c
10. b
11. c
12. b
13. c
14. b
15. b
16. a
17. c
18. a
19. c
20. b

Unit 11

1. c
2. b
3. c
4. b
5. b
6. a
7. b
8. c
9. c
10. a
11. b
12. a
13. a
14. b
15. c
16. c
17. a
18. c
19. c
20. b

Unit 12

1. c
2. b
3. a
4. b
5. a
6. a
7. b
8. c
9. b
10. a
11. a
12. c
13. b
14. c
15. a
16. a
17. c
18. a
19. a
20. b

Unit 13

1. b
2. c
3. a
4. b
5. a
6. b
7. b
8. a
9. b
10. b
11. c
12. c
13. b
14. c
15. b
16. a
17. a
18. a
19. b
20. a

Unit 14

1. b
2. b
3. b
4. c
5. c
6. a
7. a
8. b
9. c
10. c
11. c
12. a
13. c
14. a
15. a
16. b
17. c
18. b
19. a
20. c

Unit 15

1. c
2. a
3. b
4. c
5. a
6. c
7. b
8. a
9. b
10. c
11. b
12. c
13. c
14. a
15. b
16. c
17. a
18. b
19. c
20. a

Teacher Resources

Placement Test

This is an easy-to-administer screening placement test. It is designed to help you place students in the appropriate Grammar in Action Book. Remember, it is always easier to move a student up to a higher level than down to a lower level. You may wish to give students the placement test at the beginning of the term at a general testing location or in each class.

PLACEMENT GUIDE

If student scores the following on the Section 1 Placement Test:

0–10	Place in the Basic Level
10–15	Place in Level 1
15–20	Give Section 2 of the Placement Test

If student scores the following on the Section 2 Placement Test:

0–10	Place in Level 1
10–15	Place in Level 2
15–20	Give Section 3 of the Placement Test

If student scores the following on the Section 3 Placement Test:

0–10	Place in Level 2
10–15	Place in Level 3
15–20	Give Section 4 of the Placement Test

If student scores the following on the Section 4 Placement Test:

0–15	Place in Level 3
15–20	Place in a higher level series such as Grammar Dimensions

Name _____ Date _____

1. _____ is from France.

   a. Her

   b. His

   c. He

2. _____ is your name?

   a. Who

   b. What

   c. When

3. _____ this your pencil?

   a. Are

   b. Am

   c. Is

4. There are six _____ on the table.

   a. book

   b. books

   c. or books

5. I _____ in Houston.

   a. live

   b. lives

   c. living

6. Bill _____ the train.

   a. down

   b. missed

   c. overslept

7. I _____ a hat.

   a. was

   b. wore

   c. weren't

8. He _____ attention.

   a. don't pay

   b. doesn't pays

   c. doesn't pay

9. _____ you have a pen?

   a. Do

   b. Doing

   c. Does

10. _____ you take tests?

    a. Doing

    b. Do

    c. Does

11. I _____ fringe benefits.

    a. has

    b. no have

    c. don't have

12. They _____ going to the store.

    a. am

    b. is

    c. are

13. He _____ a cold.

    a. have

    b. has

    c. having

14. Mary _____ confirm her assistance.

    a. have to

    b. doesn't have to

    c. doesn't has to

15. I _____ aware of that detail.

   a. were

   b. can

   c. wasn't

16. Tim _____ in the kitchen.

   a. sit

   b. is sitting

   c. are sitting

17. They _____ letters once a month.

   a. write

   b. writes

   c. writing

18. _____ a courtyard inside the building.

   a. There are

   b. They are

   c. There is

19. You can buy food in a _____.

   a. supermarket

   b. Laundromat

   c. post office

20. The shower is in the _____.

   a. living room

   b. bathroom

   c. kitchen

Section 2

Name _____   Date _____

1. The children are standing _____ their house.

   a. from across

   b. in front

   c. across from

2. The children need to stand _____ the line.

   a. between in

   b. behind

   c. in across

3. A cook _____ food.

   a. prepares

   b. sweeps

   c. colors

4. I _____ drinking tea.

   a. are

   b. am

   c. is

5. They _____ sick.

   a. is

   b. am

   c. are

6. When he is bored, he _____ a book.

   a. reading

   b. reads

   c. read

7. Peter _____ to the radio.

   a. listen

   b. listening

   c. listens

8. They _____ twice a day.

   a. talk

   b. talking

   c. talks

9. There _____ stoplights on that street.

   a. are any

   b. aren't any

   c. is any

10. _____ are early.

   a. There

   b. It

   c. They

11. _____ heavy.

   a. There is

   b. It is

   c. They is

12. Is there a concert tonight? No, there _____.

   a. isn't

   b. aren't

   c. is

13. _____ you just get your hair cut five minutes ago?

   a. Didn't

   b. Don't

   c. Doesn't

14. She _____ her new job yesterday.

   a. starts

   b. started

   c. start

15. _____ putting on their winter clothes.

   a. They's

   b. They're

   c. They

16. When are Gordon and Helen _____ married?

   a. going to start

   b. going to get

   c. going to take

17. I am _____ buy a new car.

   a. going to

   b. went to

   c. wanting

18. I _____ in that office for fifteen years.

   a. working

   b. worked

   c. was worked

19. My mother _____ a beautiful painting.

   a. boughted

   b. buyed

   c. bought

20. When we go outside, we _____ our coats and mittens.

   a. put off

   b. put on

   c. put in

Section 3

1. _____ names are Carl and Fred.
   a. They've
   b. Their
   c. Her

2. I take walks _____ the park.
   a. in
   b. on
   c. during

3. She cooks _____.
   a. a day every
   b. every day
   c. day time every

4. There _____ empty boxes in the parking lot.
   a. is a
   b. are a
   c. are some

5. The house _____ small.
   a. was
   b. were
   c. are

6. _____ big is the house?
   a. Where
   b. How
   c. What

7. This medicine _____ bitter.
   a. tastes
   b. has tasting
   c. tasting

8. _____ everyone here today?
   a. Are
   b. Is
   c. Can

9. Would you _____ me a pen? I forgot mine.
   a. borrow
   b. borrows
   c. lend

10. He's _____ an actor.
    a. going to be
    b. going to talk
    c. getting to

11. I _____ my last car for six years.
    a. driven
    b. drove
    c. drive

12. I hope _____ a giraffe on the safari.
    a. to see
    b. seeing
    c. saw

13. I _____ a shower every morning.
    a. takes
    b. take
    c. makes

14. The little boy _____ the tall fence.
    a. climbed in
    b. climbed over
    c. climbed into

15. The police _____ the thieves.

    a. catched

    b. caught

    c. caughted

16. _____ you ever eaten sushi?

    a. Have

    b. How

    c. Did

17. They _____ music lessons.

    a. hope to begin

    b. hope begin the children's

    c. hope the children begins

18. Don't worry _____ my mother.

    a. into

    b. about

    c. to

19. The circus animals _____ by train.

    a. is transported

    b. transports

    c. are transported

20. The house _____ in a week.

    a. will be completed

    b. is be complete

    c. is completes

Section 4

1. When _____ she do her homework?
   a. do
   b. don't
   c. does

2. No one _____ any matches.
   a. having
   b. have
   c. has

3. Will you _____ me with my application?
   a. speak
   b. help
   c. show

4. _____ be the new spokesperson?
   a. Who will
   b. What will
   c. Where will

5. Ana _____ on the telephone for hours.
   a. talking
   b. talk
   c. talks

6. _____ is studying to be a doctor?
   a. Where
   b. What
   c. Who

7. Which subway station is the _____?
   a. most convenient
   b. convenientest
   c. convenient

8. How _____ does that cost?
   a. more
   b. much
   c. many

9. No, she _____.
   a. weren't
   b. wasn't
   c. was

10. Johnny _____ the flu.
    a. might have
    b. is have
    c. have

11. You _____ get a proper contract.
    a. need to
    b. wanting
    c. have better

12. It _____ cost so much to get a passport.
    a. shouldn't
    b. have better
    c. better

13. _____ you watched the news today?
    a. Has
    b. Have
    c. Hadn't

14. We have been living in this house _____ ten years.
    a. for
    b. during
    c. last

15. _____ a car is a responsibility.

 a. To drive

 b. Drive

 c. Driven

16. My parents _____ me to go back to school.

 a. pursued

 b. persuaded

 c. ask

17. The doctor expects you _____ on time.

 a. arriving

 b. arrival

 c. to arrive

18. The dissertation _____ by the committee.

 a. was approved

 b. approval

 c. approves

19. Miami, _____ is in the state of Florida, is not the capital.

 a. who

 b. where

 c. which

20. David, _____ house we went to last week, is sick.

 a. who

 b. whose

 c. which

Placement Test — Answer Key

Section 1

1. c
2. b
3. c
4. b
5. a
6. b
7. b
8. c
9. a
10. b
11. c
12. c
13. b
14. b
15. c
16. b
17. a
18. c
19. a
20. b

Section 2

1. c
2. b
3. a
4. b
5. c
6. b
7. c
8. a
9. b
10. c
11. b
12. a
13. a
14. b
15. b
16. b
17. a
18. b
19. c
20. b

Section 3

1. b
2. a
3. b
4. c
5. a
6. b
7. a
8. b
9. c
10. a
11. b
12. a
13. b
14. b
15. b
16. a
17. a
18. b
19. c
20. a

Section 4

1. c
2. c
3. b
4. a
5. c
6. c
7. a
8. b
9. b
10. a
11. a
12. a
13. b
14. a
15. a
16. b
17. c
18. a
19. c
20.

Student Checklist

Name _____ Date _____

	Comments
Listening:	
Did I listen and understand what was said?	
Did I look at others when listening?	
Speaking:	
Did I speak clearly in formal situations?	
Did I speak clearly in informal situations?	
Did I ask questions when I didn't understand something?	
Did I correct myself when speaking?	
Did I pronounce sounds and words correctly?	
Grammar:	
Did I notice when I heard incorrect grammar?	
Did I notice when I read incorrect grammar?	
Did I correct myself when using basic grammar?	
Writing:	
Did I write my name, date, and title on the page?	
Did I capitalize names of people and special places?	
Did I start every sentence with a capital letter?	
Did I use periods, question marks, and exclamation points?	
Did I indent the first line of each paragraph?	
Other:	

Notes

Notes

Notes

Notes